SELF-POWERMENT

SELF-POWERMENT

Towards a
New Way of Living

FAYE MANDELL

DUTTON

DUTTON
Published by Penguin Group (USA) Inc.
375 Hudson Street, New York, New York 10014, U.S.A.
Penguin Books Ltd, Registered Offices: 80 Strand, London WC2R 0RL, England
Penguin Books Australia Ltd, 250 Camberwell Road, Camberwell, Victoria 3124, Australia
Penguin Books Canada Ltd, 10 Alcorn Avenue, Toronto, Ontario, Canada M4V 3B2
Penguin Books (NZ) Ltd, Cnr Rosedale and Airborne Roads,
Albany, Auckland 1310, New Zealand

Published by Dutton, a member of Penguin Group (USA) Inc.

First Dutton printing, September 2003
1   3   5   7   9   10   8   6   4   2

Originally published in Canada by Namaste Publishing Inc., 2002 (n)

 REGISTERED TRADEMARK—MARCA REGISTRADA

LIBRARY OF CONGRESS CATALOGING-IN-PUBLICATION DATA

Mandell, Faye.
Self-powerment : towards a new way of living / by Faye Mandell.
p. cm.
Includes bibliographical references.
ISBN 0-525-94774-4 (alk. paper)
1. Self-actualization (Psychology). 2. Self-perception. I. Title.

BF637.S4M337 2003
158.1—dc21
2003043785

Printed in the United States of America
Set in Granjon

This book is printed on acid-free paper. ∞

This is a Namaste Publishing book

To those who are bold enough to consider new possibilities

Contents

Acknowledgments

This book is clearly born of partnerships created by the universe.

First and foremost is the sacred partnership that exists between me and my publisher, Connie Kellough. She is always present with energy, creativity, intelligence, and focus. She and I have a sacred contract.

Next is the partnership with James Eves, who helped me create the first version of this book.

I wish to thank all the peer reviewers who partnered with Connie and me to give wonderful edits and feedback. Many of the examples, stories, and descriptions in this book are the direct result of their extraordinary attention to detail and focus on the big picture.

I wish to thank Howard Kellough for allowing me to become a partnership of three for much of the last year as

Connie and I worked, almost daily, to present a clear and simple form of this material.

Finally, I would like to thank my family: Rachael, Zachary, and Benjamin, and their father, Mark, for giving me the space, support, and resources that enabled me to focus my energy to create this book.

I give all of you my deepest gratitude for being my partners.

Preface

As a publisher, I have no interest in just putting more words out into the world. I am interested only in offering readers significantly unique material that is life enhancing, even life altering. The content must be practical and immediately applicable. It is for these reasons I decided to publish *Self-Powerment*.

I received a telephone call from a friend who was familiar with my first publication. He urged me to consider publishing first-time author Faye Mandell. A little book came in the mail several days later. Instead of putting it in my pile of manuscripts waiting to be read, I put it on my bed stand and read it that night. The clarity and value of *Self-Powerment* had an immediate impact on me. The next morning, even before coffee, I declared to my husband, "I'm publishing another book."

Self-Powerment offers a quick way to get back to present-moment living. It contains everyday examples to help us practice, experience, and live from present-moment awareness. It, ironically, makes use of our conditioned, entrenched, compulsive mind structures to take us beyond them to the unlimited field of awareness within each of us. In other words, it meets us where most of us are and leads us into stiller, richer, healthier waters.

The principles of the new physics and modern psychology become exciting when applied to an examination of the workings of the human mind and, I believe, are potentially transformative.

At first, because Faye Mandell had been working with her unique self-awareness and communications Self-Powerment Model in the business community, and because my similar background of ten years in organizational development consulting has enabled me to understand the needs of this community, we targeted the book to that audience. When consulting, I always found it sad that so many people felt that they had to separate making a living from making a life. Initially, it was my hope that publishing this book would help to heal that separation.

However, a few early readers of the manuscript urged us not to restrict this book to the business sector, but to address it to all. They called it a Life Book with universal applicability. We listened, and in time came to agree with them.

The result is that you will find this book to be truly a Life Book—a book for everyone in human form today—but within that universal forum, we focus on showing how this Model can be specifically applied to the business sector. This is done by means of certain dialogues, examples, and one chapter devoted to this audience. We could have, indeed, added other chapters applying this Model to other life areas: conflict resolution, parenting, and creative problem solving, to name only a few. However, we chose to keep this book short, with the belief that more people will then read and thereby be reached by it.

It was challenging to edit this book. Most books lend themselves to a particular genre. And for them it is relatively easy to establish a clear organizing principle and achieve an overall vital cohesiveness. Since *Self-Powerment* proposes a new way of looking at how we think and communicate, it calls for its own unique structure. It attests to the statement, "You can't put new wine in old bottles." Not only did we need a new kind of container for this book, but we also needed to coin words that express the new perceptions and new understandings.

Always we asked, "How best can we communicate clearly?" Our answer was to use a variety of ways to assist the reader to understand and experience the content: examples, stories, illuminating quotations from reliable sources, tasks and practices for the reader, graphs, a question-and-answer section.

From the beginning of the book until the end, we hear Faye's unique voice guide us as she would if we were in one of her workshops. She conveys her message sincerely and in practical language.

My work as a publisher provides a special gift: the opportunity to work closely and soulfully with my authors during the prepublication process and to become authentic friends thereafter. With Faye Mandell, I encountered a commitment to her work that is singular. Atypical in a publisher-author relationship, it was she who wanted to hurry, hurry this book to press. Faye comes from the maelstromlike energy of the eastern seaboard in the United States, and I now know what it means when someone wants something done "in a New York minute." So, I am happy to finally release this book, even if, much to the frustration of its author, it took its own time to come into being.

—Connie Kellough
President, Namaste Publishing Inc.

Addendum to Preface

Shortly after the publication of *Self-Powerment* in Canada, Faye Mandell and I were introduced by Bill Gladstone, Namaste Publishing's literary agent, to Dutton, a division of Penguin Group (USA) Inc. What followed was an offer to publish *Self-Powerment* in the United States. Our objective was to have this book reach the broadest reading audience as soon as possible, and within a few weeks, we had our agreement in place. Once again, our golden web of inclusion had grown.

The wisdom and power of partnering with a skilled and supportive party in this important work became evident. Brian Tart, Vice President and Editorial Director at Dutton, was a delight to deal with at his cyberspace negotiating table. His ability to truly "hear" our concerns, his responsiveness, and his warm and consummate professionalism were compelling ingredients for our work together.

Dutton demonstrated to us that they were open to working with a mustard seed publishing house like ours. They acknowledged and valued the purpose and imprint of Namaste Publishing. Sincere and open relationships were born immediately. The flow of information back and forth was swift and efficient. All of this reinforced my experiences with our other publishing partners: for success in the workplace, beyond the capital needed for the venture, the only three requisites are a joining in common purpose, healthy relationships, and sharing of information.

Amy Hughes, the Dutton editor of *Self-Powerment,* immediately expressed an enthusiasm for and understanding of the book that exceeded my expectations. She suggested additional edits to the first edition—all of them excellent. Because of her participation, the Dutton edition of *Self-Powerment* is significantly enhanced.

It is truly a blessing to have the opportunity to join in a partnership that reinforces a consciousness that is needed on the planet at this time. This new consciousness rejects ego-based separation and competition. It seeks to join together for healthy and noble purposes.

—Connie Kellough
President, Namaste Publishing Inc.

A Modern Parable

Once upon this current time, there is Every Person, who lives a limited life—a life predominantly of striving, worrying, and never feeling good enough or achieving enough. Most of the time, EP lives in his head, dealing with his day by fretting about the future, having regrets about the past, and fantasizing about what could be. Every once in a while, however, EP experiences the security, the creativity, the completeness that make him feel truly wonderful. Then he says, "Now, this is how we are supposed to live!" It is as if he hears a familiar bell signaling to him that he has arrived home. These occasions are rare, however.

One day, in a rare and most enjoyable moment, he suddenly finds himself back at the office with his heavy "To Do" file, worrying about twenty things. "How do I get from the Here-Now to the office today?" he asks himself. "What happened? Why can't I just continue to enjoy this moment?"

These sincerely posed questions set him on a course of exploration and self-observation. He notes that it is his thinking that takes him out of his present contentment and into other times and places. Continuing with this self-observation, he discovers how certain feelings and thoughts work together. He notes that it is when he feels fear, anger, and guilt that he starts thinking in a way that takes him on disturbing and useless journeys away from the Here-Now. He follows this back further and finds that it is when he isn't feeling secure, in control, and adequate that he starts feeling and thinking this way. He experiments with just staying with his feelings and not allowing them to take him into thought.

Then an amazing thing happens. As EP continues in this awareness and practice, he finds he starts to experience more and more moments of just enjoying being with himself with no thought. This is so new an experience for him that he finds it hard to describe to others. The joy and ensuing benefits of this experience lead EP intentionally to go back to the Here-Now many times a day; he especially knows to go there if something or someone threatens his inner equilibrium in ways that bring up his needs to remain secure, in control, and adequate. The more often he goes back to this inner place, the more he finds his life changes in wonderful ways: he finds he comes up with creative ideas and solutions to the challenges of life as he meets them. He finds he has more energy and is able to focus on what is truly important in life. He finds he worries less and less and enjoys each moment more and more. His family, too, recognizes how much more at ease he is and how he seems to really enjoy being with them fully.

EP realizes he has made a great discovery. He feels like he has removed a central brick from a wall, and with that one brick's removal, brings down the whole limiting structure so that he can now see beyond to a new reality.

EP marvels at how his life has changed so suddenly, how he is able to toss away his worries, his feelings of inadequacy, and his artificial needs so easily. It is as if he has moved to a different territory and because of that experiences life differently. "How did I get from my former way of life to Here-Now?" he asks sincerely.

"Ah," says his muse, "this is what the book in your hand is all about."

Introduction

It's amazing. I was able to get through my whole educational experience without having taken a physics course. In my naïveté at that time, I just thought that physics was something to be feared. Physics was for smart, scientific people, not for average folks. Imagine, four years of college, a master's, and a doctorate without one physics course. After finishing my last degree, I went to work. One night I was browsing through an adult education brochure and saw a description of a course called "Quantum Physics and the Face of God." I just knew that I had to take it. I dragged two of my colleagues along, and from that day forward, my life has never been the same. Although part of the course dealt with mathematical formulas, most of it dealt with the relationship of physics to awareness. I was surprised that there was a connection between physics and psychology. It was as if a vast door unlocked, making a primal connection for me. I was hooked.

Furthermore, I had no idea that I was engaging in transformational possibilities. I didn't even know what transformational possibilities meant. I was a psychologist and was interested in helping people. I never before understood that there was another whole level, or more, of awareness that up until now had been unavailable to me.

The relationship between physics and awareness became my focus. It allowed me to shift my view of reality. We are taught certain things in our culture about what exists and what does not. Our thoughts are regarded as truth in our society. It never dawned on me to question the validity of my thoughts and my thought process as a whole. Today I can chuckle and grin at the bumper sticker that reads YOU DON'T HAVE TO BELIEVE EVERYTHING YOU THINK. However, before I could detach from my own thoughts, I spent most of my time doing just that—believing and listening to the racket of thoughts that would control my attention at all times of the day. For instance, I spent energy when out with other people, constantly comparing myself to them and finding myself inferior. Be it at work, at a party, or just in a public setting, much of my energy and focus was on my nagging insecurities or on what others might have (looks, money, talent, and so forth) that I did not. I gave time and energy to my thoughts that created these insecurities. When I looked in the mirror, I always saw the things that were wrong with me. I had a habit of creating scenarios in my head of what I should have done to look prettier or say something smarter. By doing this, I was living in the past with guilt, and I focused on others, feeling angry. While using my energy on these thoughts, which were far from productive, I believed what I then took to be fact: I would never find a meaningful relationship or great job. And by spending my time on these thoughts, I was fulfilling my own prophecy.

It never occurred to me that there were alternative ways to understand my relationship to others and myself. Teachers, friends, or other sage folk may have tried to show me this, but they made little progress because I trusted my thoughts. Along with the high value we place on thoughts, there is also a devaluation of feelings.

By going along with society's general negation of feelings, I tried to fit in, but I never felt at ease. There was a constant battle within me between what I was told was right and appropriate, and what I *felt*. I couldn't speak of these conflicting experiences, because I didn't have the words or concepts yet to do this, but I did know that I did not feel clear, focused, and at peace. As a matter of fact, I felt *dis*-ease, and this continued throughout my life until I bumped directly into the interrelationship between psychology and physics.

Now, with my new discoveries, I began to understand the uneasiness I had felt all my life. I began to see beyond my own limited perspective. There was a dimly lit recognition that I had touched upon something magical, something unknown, a virtual gateway to possibilities. I became aware that when we experience life directly in the present moment and ignore thoughts, we open to a whole new way of being. My gut feeling of what life is all about was affirmed. The shoulds, the what ifs, and the thoughts about the need to be perfect, lovable, attractive, and smart were just that—only thoughts. These are the thoughts that compare, judge, and negate. I have discovered that thoughts by themselves are different from the actual experience of living. Instead of clarifying and being helpful in practical ways, I realized that thoughts, being at least one step away from the direct experience of the present moment, can also distort, confuse, and mislead. I became aware that the fleeting glimpses of clarity, focus, ease, and gratitude I felt when experiencing life directly in the Here-Now could be expanded so that I could spend more of my life appreciating it rather than judging, comparing, negating, worrying, being angry, or feeling guilty for who I am.

These discoveries were so new and so thrilling that I felt both excitement and apprehension. Through reading, I began to explore more about this gateway of using the hard sciences, such as physics, to explore awareness. Reading from a lay perspective in physics and having, through years of schooling, a highly intellectual perspective in psychology, I felt a unique awareness of how these two disciplines can be interwoven. This awareness has led, over time, to the development of a working empirical model, which relies on the interconnectedness of the two disciplines to make practical, everyday use of both of them. *Self-Powerment* is about this Model.

The Model that is being presented in this book combines elements from the disciplines of psychology and physics. Because of the interdisciplinary nature of this Model and because new material is being presented, common terms such as *thought, feeling, time,* and *space,* among other concepts, are redefined and used in novel ways to convey the new understandings, the new awarenesses. Language always has had to adjust to accommodate our growing consciousness and changing worldview. In this book, you encounter new terms, such as *wobble, piggyback, feeling-thought, Here-Now,* and *Self-Powerment*. I define these in the new context in which I am using them. For your reference, there is a glossary at the back of the book, as well. It is best to refer to the glossary to review definitions only after you have encountered them in the text and not before.

These new words and definitions might feel a bit unusual

and alien until you become familiar with them. Try to remain open to the way they are being used in the Model. When new material is presented, we have a habit of going into judgment, comparison, and negation to avoid experiencing it. Often, we try to guard and protect our current perception of the way we believe things are. **It is fundamental to remember: as long as we are judging, we cannot fully experience changes in awareness.** Because of this, I request that for the duration of your reading of *Self-Powerment,* you suspend any impulse you might have to compare this Model to other workshops you have attended or material that you have read, and refrain from premature conclusions. A good way to do this is to recognize, identify, and avoid what I call "killer thoughts," which are thoughts about all the ways the Model *can't* work. New ideas need to live long enough to have a chance to prove their validity and worth. It is helpful to see these killer thoughts as conditioned patterns that keep you from the present moment. Watch your thought process in action. Negative thoughts, such as "This won't work for me," "I've already tried this," or "It can't be that simple," are killer thoughts. These always have a negative message that ultimately does not allow us to see clearly. Watch for these and become an aware observer of your thoughts. As I have said, see them for what they are—just thoughts. You exist apart from them.

As Eckhart Tolle said in *The Power of Now,* "The single most vital step on your journey toward enlightenment is this: learn to disidentify from your mind." This is a valuable instruction, and the Self-Powerment Model provides a practical step-by-step way in which to do this in our daily lives.

When you read, don't hurry to the conclusion. When a new term is being used or an important concept is being explained, it is a good idea to pause and let yourself *experience* it. In this book, I share with you things you already know but that have been covered up by learned ways of thinking. **When you experience a moment directly, you are returning to information that has always been within you but has been put into such artificial categories that it is no longer accessible.** For example, many children are placed in the category of "slow learners." Yet these children are gifted in so many ways. As soon as we have separated them into a category, we are unlikely to see them in their true capacity, in their fullness. This Model provides a way to bypass these artificial categories and return to direct experience in the Here-Now.

Many people have written about the benefits of living in the Here-Now; in this book, I provide a practical, simple way to do this.

One

COMMUNICATING SOME
NEW IDEAS

As a student of psychology, I found two major topics that aroused my interest: feelings and thoughts. I discuss these terms in this chapter. It is important that you be introduced to the way we use them in the Self-Powerment Model before moving on to the Model itself. Other terms that are discussed are time and space, Here-Now, the I Am, and feeling-thoughts.

When I became more skilled at listening to people, I observed that although the content of what people said varied, whenever they spoke about their worries and fears, they were always talking about the future. Whenever they talked about their regrets and guilt, they were always talking about the past. Whenever they talked about their anger, they were always focused on other people and things outside of themselves or on a very narrow aspect of themselves. The common denominator, regardless of the specific experience, was that they were speaking from a specific time-and-space perspective, and that focus was away from their direct experience of the present moment—in other words, away from the Here-Now.

I began to realize that there was something about what we label "unpleasant" feelings that made people talk about them in any way but from a Here-Now perspective. After I started to read enthusiastically and extensively in the area of physics, I experimented with how concepts like time and space can be applied to how people talk about feelings. From there, I worked on developing a model that people could use which combines some of these concepts to achieve awareness. The next section presents our working definitions of these concepts as they are used in the Self-Powerment Model.

Thought

Thinking is as natural as perceiving and behaving. We all have used phrases like, "Let's think about it," "Think before you speak," "We need to give it more thought," and "Let's try to think outside the box." The act of thinking is highly esteemed in our society. Despite this, most of us think without giving much attention to the actual thought process. The dictionary definition of thought is simply "the product of mental activity." **Yet most of us do not realize how much power our thoughts have over us. When we begin to grasp this, we can begin to shift that power so that we can use thought for our own self-powerment.**

A key to self-powerment is to observe thoughts in an objective way. It is to our advantage to become the outside observer of our mental activity and thoughts.

In the Self-Powerment Model, the different aspects of thought are introduced. We explore how we create our thoughts. **The structure of thought has two dimensions: time and space. The structure of thought tells us (1) where we are in time (that is, past, present, future) and (2) where we are in space (that is, where our attention is focused).**

When we put gelatin into a mold, it takes the form of the mold. The mold then structures the gelatin into a shape, such as a star, triangle, or circle. Gelatin is the thought and the mold is the structure that shapes the thought. Using this analogy, the mold can be seen to be the structure of the thought, which is where the thought takes us in time and space.

For example, when we go to a movie, as soon as the movie is over, when we think and talk about that experience, the thought takes us into the past, since the direct experience of it is over. We will likely talk about just a few aspects of the movie, specific fragments that caught our attention or piqued our interest, such as the plot line, a certain character, or the special effects. Even though we may try, we can never completely and accurately re-create our former direct experience of seeing the movie, since we need to rely on thoughts that are structured in the past to do so.

We call the actual experience of watching the movie direct experience. The structure of the thoughts that reference this direct experience are (1) when the movie was watched (past) and (2) where our attention is focused (on a character, the plot line, and so on). These two elements, time and space, make up the structure of the thought. After we move away from the direct experience of watching the movie, we categorize our experience with thoughts referring to the specific time and space that made up that experience. But we are always re-creating that experience with thought and never have the genuine direct experience again. Even if we watched the movie again, it may remind us of the experience we had initially, but our first watching of the movie is always unique.

By differentiating between the thought and its structure, we can separate them to determine what is real.

In the Self-Powerment Model, the structure of thought is where the thought takes us in time and space. When a thought occurs, being conscious of where we are in time (past, present, future) and where we are in space (where our attention is focused) is a new experience for most of us. Observing this gives us a new way to detach from our thoughts. Many of us have never been told that having an awareness of where we are in time and space is so important. That's what is so exciting!

Take a moment to observe some thoughts you have frequently. For example, "I will never get this done," "I'm overweight," or "I'll never find someone I love." See how these relate to the structure of thought.

Time and Space

Our working definition of time places us in the past, present, or the future. Our working definition of space lets us know where our attention is focused. In everyday terms, time and space are perceived as separate. Time is seen as a limited interval or period, and space is seen as an expanse in which material objects are located. Actually, time and space are important because they are points of reference for us. They define and shape an experience. For example, "The project will take three weeks," or "Yesterday was my father's birthday." Time and space limit and define experience. They are important concepts because they help us to locate and reference direct experience and to communicate the experience to others.

In this book, time and space take on a whole new value: they help us to locate ourselves **when we are not in the Here-Now.** In the Self-Powerment Model, time and space are seen as a continuum. In *The Dancing Wu Li Masters*, Gary Zukav says of a continuum, it is "something whose parts are so close together, so arbitrarily small that the continuum really cannot be broken down into them. There are no breaks in continuum." In other words, time and space are experienced as one in a continuum. Together they provide a compass for navigating to our place of Self-Powerment.

As used in this model, time and space are universal reference points that allow us to enter the gateway to direct experience. Remember *Alice's Adventures in Wonderland!* She opens each door and finds herself in a different time and space. We do the same when we open a door to the past or future and shift our focus to other people or things. We leave where we are at the present moment and visit another timespace with thoughts like, "Yesterday was my father's birthday."

Structurally learned patterns of thought take us out of the present moment. As a society, we use learned patterns of thought frequently. When doing this, we leave the Here-Now without consciously choosing to do so. This is why it is important to observe our thoughts regularly.

Here-Now and I Am

Being in the present moment, without thought, is being in the Here-Now. The Here-Now is where we access direct experience. It is where we experience consciousness without thought. Another way to define Here-Now is I Am. To be in the I Am is to be fully in the present moment with attention focused on our internal multisensory experience. These two terms, Here-Now and I Am go hand in hand. As you can see, Here-Now and I Am reference time and space. I Am is the way Here-Now is expressed in our language. It is the way we associate ourselves with time and space. **I Am defines us in time and space.**

SPACE	TIME
HERE	NOW
I	AM

The columns above show how we can make practical use of the concepts of space and time to position ourselves in the Here-Now, which is expressed in our language by the words "I Am."

To be in the I Am is the most wondrous state because it is in the I Am that we experience our authentic self. It is the only place where we know what is so. Fear, anger, and guilt no longer create our reality. Our mind is free of structurally learned patterns of thought. We are not subjected to or limited by the learned patterns of thought, which force us to judge, evaluate, compare, and negate, and leave the Here-Now. Indeed, we are free to experience the Here-Now in its fullness. **In the I Am, all the blending, folding, shaping, textures, and nuances of life operate perfectly.** We are fully present, aware, and at peace. We are free to create from infinite possibilities. In the I Am, the wisdom housed in our very cells is available to us. We can experience without the encumbrance of the artificial boundaries that thought imposes. We have access to the vast array of sensory information that is not clouded or limited by thought. There are so many gifts we have when we are fully in the Here-Now.

When we are in the I Am, we are able to focus on our talents or work. We focus our talents, be it on work, the person we are with, the task we are doing, or just being. This is the time-space in which our true creativity and full potential emerge.

I am not the first person to know that the Here-Now, the I Am, is the place where people are self-powered. We see the I Am when Tiger Woods plays golf, Michael Jordan plays basketball, Mark McGwire plays baseball, or Venus and Serena Williams play tennis. We experience it when our child is hurt and we go into the immediate right action or when we call a parent or relative spontaneously because we just know something is wrong. We call it the "zone." When we are in the zone, we access data from direct experience with an expanded sensory database.

In the zone, we are able to intuit our experience totally. We are self-powered. We are aware of the extraordinary amount and variation of information accessible from our senses.

Once, after taking attendance when teaching a course to college freshmen, I asked, "Who is really present? I mean whose attention is focused in this room at this time, as opposed to being somewhere else in time and space: for example, reliving a fight you had with your boyfriend last night, worrying about an assignment that is due tomorrow, or trying to figure out how you are ever going to pay back your loan for college tuition and such?" I reminded them that since I was a guest lecturer, their response would not affect their grades. Out of the forty-five students, not one could truly admit that their focus was on being in the class at that moment.

Feelings

Feelings play a large role in our life. **A feeling is a physical sensation. It is experienced in the Here-Now and has no thought component. Feelings are nature's indicators that one of our emotional needs must be attended to. Feelings are the fundamental tools that nature gives us for staying in the Here-Now.** Feelings allow us to stay in balance. They allow us to be aware of both our strengths and weaknesses. **In the Self-Powerment Model, we focus on three of these feelings: anxiety, frustration, and disappointment/sadness.** For example, when we have a half-completed report due at three o'clock, and it's already two o'clock, we experience a feeling—anxiety—that allows us to focus and stay present with the task at hand to complete it and feel secure that we are doing our job competently. When we experience frustration and disappointment at the end of an emotional relationship, these feelings allow us to *know* it is over and let us take accountability for our part in the ending of the relationship.

Feelings emerge in response to experiences, such as missing the bus, having a flight cancelled, getting a divorce, or receiving a demotion. We learn to ignore these feelings because they are not valued and often not acceptable in our society. We demean natural feelings and avoid experiencing them. Everyone knows the cliché "Men don't cry." Generally, feelings are not communicated in our society and are often treated by denial.

Feelings are the fundamental tool that nature gives as for staying in the Here-Now—for staying self-powered. Feelings are physical sensations that are experienced in the Here-Now. Natural feelings maintain balance, clarity, focus, control, and self-confidence.

Feeling-Thoughts

As seen in the previous section, we often do not allow ourselves to experience feelings. However, feelings occur all the time. Because we are not allowed to experience them, we have had to find a way to discharge them. We have learned to link them with a thought to discharge them.

As we discharge our feelings, we automatically associate a thought with a feeling. We may see them as partners in crime. **We link feelings to our thoughts, and by doing this we create a feeling-thought.** When this occurs, we lose the experience of the natural feeling.

A feeling-thought is defined as a feeling that has been so inextricably bound up with thought, that the pure experience of the feeling can no longer be distinguished from the thought. Compare it to making batter by mixing milk with eggs: soon you are no longer able to see the milk separate from the egg. After a feeling has been combined with a thought, it is no longer possible to experience the feeling as separate.

As in the previous example, we often do not allow ourselves to experience the frustration and disappointment in the ending of a relationship. Instead, we might blame the other person and continue to focus on the "should haves," "could haves," and "would haves." When we do this, we are no longer able to distinguish the thoughts from the feelings.

For instance, when we point out, "That's his house," to identify the exact location of a residence, we can experience "his house" as the stage for our personal drama if internally we are thinking, "That's his house where five years ago he told me he wanted a divorce." In this way, we experience the divorce over and over again, attaching the feelings of frustration and sadness to the event.

So how can we know the difference between thought and feeling? Remember that the experience of a feeling is a physical sensation with no thought component. Initially, the frustration and disappointment were natural feelings without a thought. In a nanosecond, we discharged them by linking them to thoughts of blame or should have, could have, and would have. **By listening to the structure of the thoughts—that is where those thoughts take us in time-space—we can reference ourselves in time-space and reconnect to the natural feeling.** It is a remarkable awakening to experience consciousness without thought. This is possible when we learn to distinguish between thought and feeling.

Take a moment. How do you deal with your feelings on a regular basis?

* * *

A feeling links with a thought taking us out of the Here-Now, **without choice. This is the reason we create structurally learned patterns of thought—to discharge those feelings that we do not allow expression.** Possibly, as a way to identify ourselves as uniquely human or to separate ourselves from lower species, we have come to discount the importance of feelings and to exalt thought. We must remember that feelings are very real. We may ignore them, but they remain with us, only to surface at another time when they, once again, try to get our attention.

This Model allows us to remember what we already know but have not been encouraged to experience. When we don't fully experience our feelings, we become disenfranchised from our own inner and authentic power. When we reconnect to the place where we are fully immersed in experiencing our natural feelings, we are able to open to compassion, connection, conjoinment, integrity, and love. We experience the fullness of life and naturally express our gratitude for the ongoing gift of it.

Time and space are universal reference points, which are indispensable to civilized society. They have tremendous practical value. They help us function on a daily basis: to schedule and attend medical appointments, work meetings, and dinner engagements. They are necessary for the mechanical processes of life, such as preparing a menu or building a house. They help us to establish ownership: my car, your book, or his problem. In addition, they create the forum in which we do long-term planning: for example, I will get my degree in three years from the university. However, over the thousands of years of human conditioning, we have come to expand the use of time and space. They now serve an additional function to structure our thoughts, which then become the vehicles to discharge personal feelings by reverting to the past, speculating on the future, or focusing outside ourselves and away from the present moment.

By using nouns, pronouns, and verbs—the time and space words in our language—and linking them to the discharge of feelings, we personalize time and space. Time and space become meshed with feelings. When we combine time, space, and feelings, we lose the practical benefits of time and space, and the ability to stay in the Here-Now.

The next chapter presents the Self-Powerment Model. This Model allows us to create a mental picture of where we are in time and space. Are we in the past, in the present, in the future? Are we focusing on other people and things? Are we looking only at a fragment of ourselves? This internal picture becomes the means to connect to and experience our natural feelings, which guide us into self-powerment. Just asking ourselves, "Where am I? Who or what else is with me? Am I seeing only a fragment of myself? Am I only listening to thoughts that dwell on the past and future?" brings a new way to identify if we are in the I Am. This simple inquiry is very powerful. When we pay attention to the structure of a thought, we can choose to observe what the focus of the thought is—that is, on others or only on a fragment of ourselves—as well as where the thought takes us in time-space. And once we have this awareness, we can choose to eliminate those thoughts that cause unease and dissipate our energy.

Two

THE SELF-POWERMENT MODEL
It's All about Choice

In the last chapter, we established that we create structurally learned patterns of thought to discharge those
feelings we avoid experiencing. When we can free ourselves
from these patterns and return to direct experience, we open
to the infiniteness of possibilities and can exercise our free
choice regarding how we want to participate in our lives.

Before I introduce the Self-Powerment Model, try this
exercise. Think about eating a piece of chocolate. Describe
that experience; write it down on a piece of paper. Then eat
a piece of chocolate, preferably an M&M's candy. Now write
down that experience. Note the vastly different information
that is accessed when you *think* about something versus
when you experience it directly.

Thinking about your dream vacation is very different
from experiencing it. When you actually take the vacation,
you may experience it as even better than you anticipated, or

you may be disappointed. But at least through experience, you find out what is so!

The Self-Powerment Model presented here allows you the choice to access direct experience.

We all have biological needs. We also have indicators that let us know these needs exist. When we are hungry, our stomach growls and we get stomach pains. If we didn't listen to this indicator, we would die. When we are thirsty, we lick our lips, our mouth gets dry, and we get something to drink. When we are sleepy, our eyelids droop, we yawn, and we lie down and go to sleep.

Just as we have biological needs, we also have emotional needs. **These needs are to be secure, in control, and adequate.** When these are being met, we are in the Here-Now—the I Am. I represent these needs on a time and space graph.

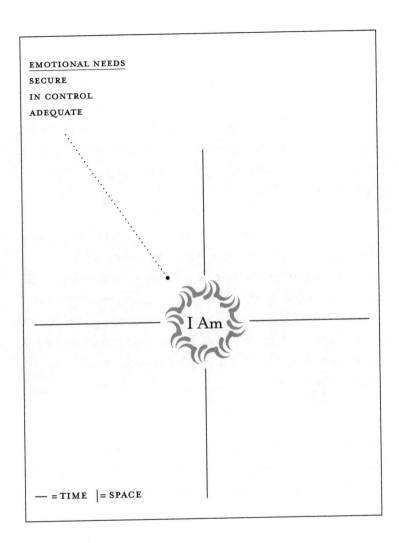

EMOTIONAL NEEDS
SECURE
IN CONTROL
ADEQUATE

I Am

— = TIME | = SPACE

Time-Space Referent

In the last chapter, I introduced time and space as the building blocks for the Self-Powerment Model. The horizontal line represents time, and the vertical line represents space. It is at the intersection where the time and space lines meet that we feel secure, in control, and adequate. We represent this in our language by the words *I Am*. *Am* is a present-tense verb that lets us know we are in the present, and *I* is a pronoun that lets us know that our energy is focused on our **intuition, wisdom, and ken:** our multisensory data.

For our purposes, *intuition* is the direct perception of the truth. *Wisdom* is the direct information encoded in our DNA that provides us with the process to be human. *Ken* is our range of sight or vision. It means to have knowledge about or to know. The ability to consider one's range of sight at all times is ken.

The following are some graphs to help you observe when you leave the Here-Now. They create an internal map to assist you to observe how the structure of your thoughts can take you out of the I Am. This internal "treasure" map can guide you back to accessing direct experience.

Future

When we go out on the time line to the right, we go to the future. Some of the words that let us know we are in the future are *will, could, should, might,* and *what if*.

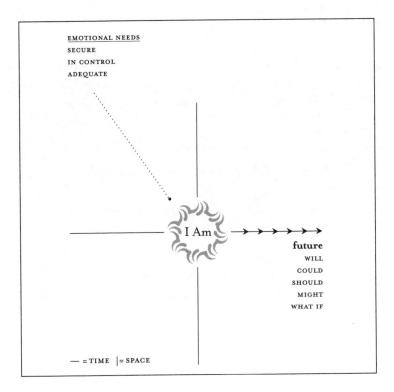

Examples:

"I will never get it done."

"What if my husband loses his job?"

Take a moment to consider how often you use the words, *will, could, should, might,* and *what if*. Are these words accompanied by a feeling of unease?

Past

When we go on the time line to the left, we go to the past. Some of the words that let us know we are in the past are *did, had, was, could have, would have,* and *should have*.

Examples:

"If I would have gone to college, I could have gotten a better job."

"If I could have taken the trip, I might have met the man of my dreams."

Take a moment to consider how often you use these words: *did, had, was, could have, would have,* and *should have*. Are these words accompanied by a feeling of unease?

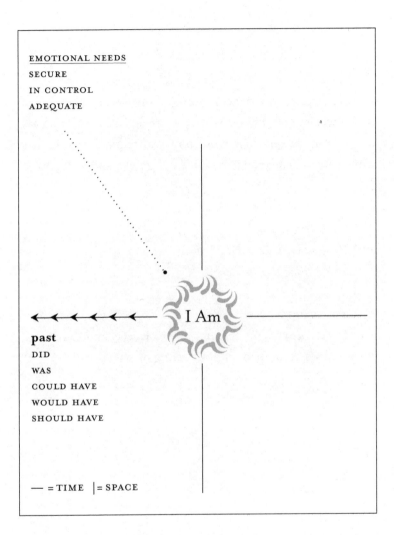

EMOTIONAL NEEDS
SECURE
IN CONTROL
ADEQUATE

I Am

←←←←←←

past
DID
WAS
COULD HAVE
WOULD HAVE
SHOULD HAVE

— = TIME | = SPACE

Create Others and Things

When we go up on the space line, we create other people, situations, and experiences. Some of the words that let us know we are creating other people are *he, she, they,* and *you.* Some of the words that let us know we are focusing on other things are *the budget, the deadline, the grades,* and so forth.

Examples:

"*You're being mean.*"

"*The deadline is unrealistic.*"

"*He is causing this disaster.*"

Take a moment to consider how often you use these words: *he, she, you, the deadline, the mortgage,* and so on. Are these words accompanied by a feeling of unease?

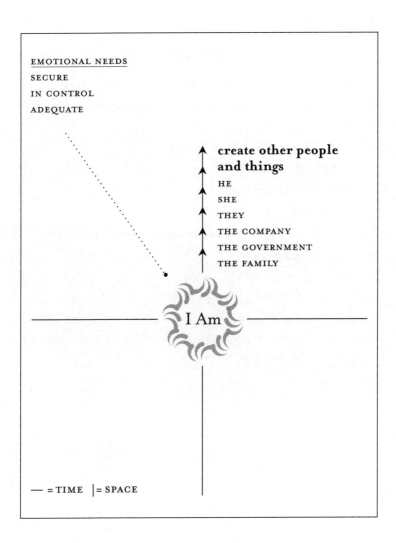

EMOTIONAL NEEDS
SECURE
IN CONTROL
ADEQUATE

create other people
and things
HE
SHE
THEY
THE COMPANY
THE GOVERNMENT
THE FAMILY

I Am

— = TIME | = SPACE

Distort

When we go down the space line, we take a fragment of our self-image and magnify it to become our whole identity.

Examples:
"*I'm not smart enough.*"
"*I'm not strong enough.*"
"*I'm too old.*"
"*I know this stuff better than anyone; everyone else around here is incompetent.*"

Observe that going up or down the space line is, in both instances, merely focusing away from ourselves and getting away from what is experienced internally, or focusing on only a part of ourselves.

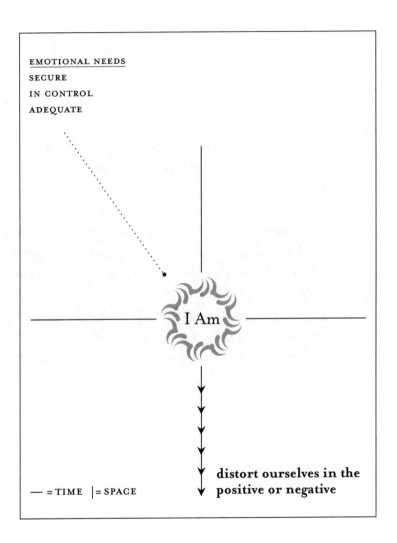

EMOTIONAL NEEDS
SECURE
IN CONTROL
ADEQUATE

I Am

— = TIME | = SPACE

distort ourselves in the
positive or negative

Feelings in the Self-Powerment Model

In the Self-Powerment Model, when a feeling indicates that an emotional need must be attended to, we call that state being in **wobble.**

Just as we have indicators that let us know our biological needs are in wobble, we also have indicators that let us know our emotional needs are in wobble. These indicators are called *feelings*. As I have said before, nature gives us feelings for a reason. Inherent in the experience of a feeling is the action we need to take in order to feel secure, in control, and adequate—an action that enables us to stay self-powered in the Here-Now.

As mentioned earlier, a feeling is a physiological sensation that has no thought component. We can liken it to our stomach growling or our mouth getting dry. It is a biological indicator that signals us to do something to stay in the Here-Now. In the Self-Powerment Model,

- The feeling that lets us know our security need is in wobble is **anxiety.**
- The feeling that lets us know our control need is in wobble is **frustration.**
- The feeling that lets us know our adequacy need is in wobble is **disappointment** or **sadness.**

A natural feeling occurs in the present moment. When we focus our attention on it, it is a storehouse of essential information that is felt and processed and gives meaning simultaneously. It is our most immediate and authentic response. Each of the three natural feelings that the Self-Powerment Model addresses provide the energy that signals that we must interact with our environment in some way to stay Self-Powered.

Let's Look at How These Feelings Work

When we are focused inside ourselves, we rely on our own intuition, wisdom, and ken. If we are still and allow no thoughts to intrude, we can understand why we have learned to avoid our feelings in their pure state. In order to regain the ability to experience our feelings, we have to look at how our feelings have become conditioned. And to do this, we need to go to our early childhood to see how this happened.

First, let's look at anxiety. A little girl comes home from school and says, "Mommy and Daddy, I'm so worried about a test I have tomorrow. It's one third of my grade, and I really want to do well. I'm so nervous."

Like all parents, Mommy and Daddy have learned that they do not want their daughter to be anxious. They might say, "Don't worry, honey. We'll help you study and do a good job. Please don't be anxious." The feeling is avoided by an immediate solution provided by the parents.

Let's now turn to frustration. Johnny comes home from a baseball game his team has lost and says to his parents, "I'm so frustrated. Our baseball team lost every game this season. I guess we don't practice enough. I'm just so frustrated." His parents might say, "Don't be frustrated. We'll help you practice after school and talk to the coach about practicing more often." Again, there is the strong negation of the experience of the feeling, in this case, frustration.

Finally, let's look at disappointment and sadness. Sally comes home and says, "Mary's having a party. She's invited all the other girls, but not me. I'm so sad and disappointed."

The parents take away Sally's feeling of sadness immediately. They might say, "Don't be sad. We'll make a bigger party with balloons and clowns, and won't invite Mary."

After years of repeated reinforcement that feelings are not acceptable, we have learned not to feel them. For most of us, our conditioning, or learned patterns of thought, has created an impenetrable barrier, denying us access to direct experience. Like the children in the above examples, we have learned not to experience our feelings. But feelings cannot be eliminated. And the problem is that once a feeling is evoked, it must be discharged. Let's take a look at how this works.

Feeling-Thought: Fear

If a feeling can't be discharged by experiencing it, the feeling moves from the body to a thought. It is piggybacked and gets discharged that way. **In this Model, to piggyback is to take a feeling and move it from the body onto a thought.** The act of moving a feeling, which belongs in the body, to a thought, takes us out of the Here-Now, out of our place of Self-Powerment. As we know, a feeling-thought is the combination that results when a feeling gets connected to a thought in a nanosecond—that is, it is piggybacked onto a thought.

Remember, when a feeling seeps into the thought, the result of that seepage is that we must structure the thought in a particular way. That means that the thought must take a particular form or a particular structure, similar to the mold that shapes the gelatin into a star, triangle, or circle.

We can all see how common feeling-thoughts are in our daily lives. For example, Tom has a project due at 3:00 P.M., and because there is still a lot to do, he begins to feel anxiety. That anxiety, when used naturally, allows him to stay focused, clear, and in touch with his creativity, wisdom, and ken. However, he has learned to take that anxiety, and in a nanosecond, piggyback it onto a thought, which takes him into the future, namely, "I'll never get this job done in time.

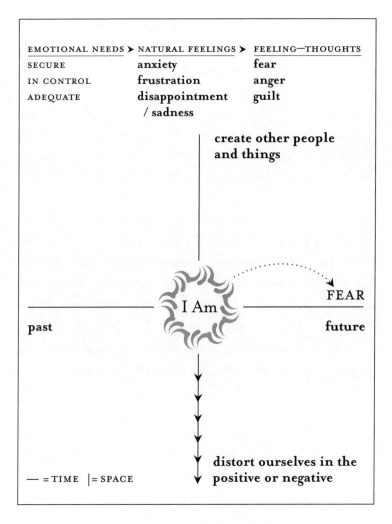

EMOTIONAL NEEDS ➤	NATURAL FEELINGS ➤	FEELING—THOUGHTS
SECURE	anxiety	fear
IN CONTROL	frustration	anger
ADEQUATE	disappointment / sadness	guilt

create other people
and things

I Am

FEAR

past

future

distort ourselves in the
positive or negative

— = TIME | = SPACE

They won't ever give me another opportunity to prove my capability." Now we have this new combination of a feeling-thought. **The feeling-thought of anxiety is fear.**

We can see this in all sorts of situations. For instance, when Rachel's boyfriend says he will be at her house at 8:00 P.M., Rachel prepares for his arrival and time passes. He is late. It is 10 P.M., and he still hasn't arrived. Carried away by her thoughts, Rachel has already decided that he is with another woman and is coming back only to tell her he is leaving her forever. This is another scenario in which the feeling of anxiety becomes the feeling-thought of fear.

Feelings can also attach themselves to behaviors and lead to phobias, addictions, and overly aggressive acts toward other people. This topic, however, is beyond the scope of this book.

Anxiety is what allows us to keep our attention on what is important in the moment. This focus allows us to do what is necessary to stay secure. When we find ourselves forced into the future, we have piggybacked the feeling of anxiety *onto a thought*. When we piggyback the feeling, we create thoughts meshed with anxiety, and they are experienced as thoughts in the future. We know we are in the future when we use words like *will, never, what if, always, might,* and so forth. Most, if not all, of the energy needed to get the task done is used, instead, to move the feeling of anxiety and create the structure of thought about the future. These thoughts remove us from the present, where we are able to use that anxiety to focus and to access the creative resources we need to deal with the experience in the present.

Feeling-Thought: Anger

In the following scenario, one of Shirley's children, Karen, spills some of her red finger paint onto a white carpet. As a result, Shirley feels frustrated and out of control. Rather than find the carpet cleaner or call the carpet cleaning company, Shirley begins to yell at Karen and blame her for her carelessness. Instead of experiencing the frustration which would immediately lead to cleaning the carpet, she piggybacks that frustration onto a thought, shifts the focus to her daughter, and blames her for her carelessness.

In another example, Bob places an urgent call and reaches an answering machine. Instead of using his frustration to stay in control and do something available to him, such as returning e-mails, or using his energy to do productive work while waiting to speak with the person he is attempting to reach, his frustration gets piggybacked and is experienced as, "What a jerk that guy is. Why isn't he ever there when I want him? He's always unavailable to me!" Rather than feeling the frustration, Bob piggybacks it onto a thought. The feeling moves from the body to a thought, seeps into the thought, and requires that Bob structure the thought about blaming other people and things. **The feeling-thought of frustration is anger.**

Frustration lets us know that we are out of control, not

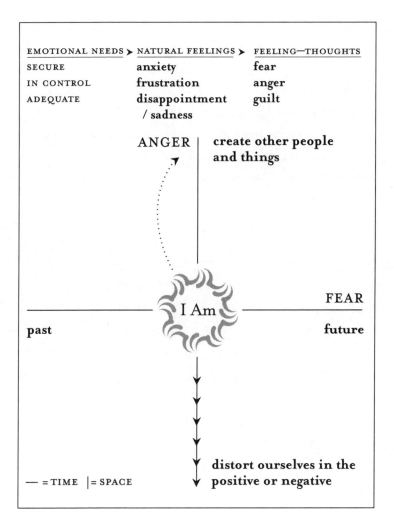

EMOTIONAL NEEDS ➤ NATURAL FEELINGS ➤ FEELING—THOUGHTS

EMOTIONAL NEEDS	NATURAL FEELINGS	FEELING—THOUGHTS
SECURE	anxiety	fear
IN CONTROL	frustration	anger
ADEQUATE	disappointment / sadness	guilt

ANGER | create other people and things

I Am

FEAR

past | future

— = TIME | = SPACE

distort ourselves in the positive or negative

the situation. When we find ourselves focusing on other people, situations, and experiences, creating them in our head without choice, we have piggybacked frustration, which is our indicator to get back into control. We create thoughts meshed with frustration and the structure of the thoughts is experienced as thoughts about other people or things. We know that we are creating other people and things when we use words like *he, she, they, you, them, those,* and so forth. **The feeling-thought is anger.**

Feeling-Thought: Guilt

In the following situation, Jane is a high school senior and is rejected from her first choice in universities. Rather than feeling the disappointment and recognizing all her other options, she goes to the past and thinks about all the things she didn't do in high school that could have made a difference in the admissions process to her first choice university. Here her disappointment and sadness are piggybacked onto a thought and become guilt.

In another example, Linda makes a mistake at work, causing a major project to fall a month behind schedule. Instead of using her disappointment to complete the experience and learn from it, she piggybacks the feeling. It is then experienced as thoughts with the focus on the past, such as, "I should have asked for help," or "I could have done more research."

This work situation evokes disappointment or sadness, and rather than feeling it, Linda piggybacks it onto a thought. The feeling moves from the body to a thought, seeps into the thought, and requires that she create a thought about the past. **The feeling-thought of disappointment/sadness is guilt.**

Sadness or disappointment lets us know that we need to address the reality of endings. When we find ourselves in

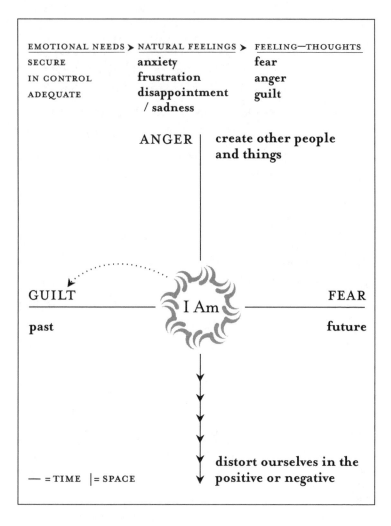

EMOTIONAL NEEDS ➤	NATURAL FEELINGS ➤	FEELING—THOUGHTS
SECURE	anxiety	fear
IN CONTROL	frustration	anger
ADEQUATE	disappointment / sadness	guilt

ANGER | create other people and things

GUILT   I Am   FEAR

past   future

— = TIME | = SPACE

distort ourselves in the positive or negative

the past without choice, we have piggybacked the feeling of sadness or disappointment, which is our indicator that lets us know there is no real connection between loss and adequacy. We create thoughts meshed with sadness, and we experience the structures of these thoughts in the past. We know we are in the past when we use words like *should have, could have, would have, done, had, was,* and *did.*

These thoughts take us away from the present, where we can use the sadness to complete the experience and keep perspective. **The feeling-thought is guilt.**

Distortion Is the Foundation

When we leave the Here-Now *without conscious choice,* and go to the future or the past, or create other people or experiences, we simultaneously distort ourselves in the positive or the negative. The structure of the distortion is that we look at ourselves either positively or negatively in an exaggerated way. We lose our capacity to keep a balanced perspective of our strengths and weaknesses, so one strength or weakness can be taken for our whole identity at the time.

For example, "I'm not smart enough," "I don't have enough education," or "I am the only one who can do this; the others aren't competent."

When we go there directly, we experience negative self-talk. We go there directly when we are frustrated with ourselves and turn that frustration into a judgment of ourselves. We go there indirectly when the situation or other people become the basis for the judgment, comparison, or negation.

The distortion half of the space line is joined with one of the other three feeling-thoughts: fear, anger, and guilt.

Natural Feelings

In the Self-Powerment Model, fear, anger, and guilt are not natural, pure feelings, but distortions of them that result from the natural feeling being piggybacked onto a thought. When feelings and thoughts are meshed together, neither can be used as nature intended. The feelings of anxiety, frustration, and disappointment/sadness are indicators to let us know that we must do something to reconnect to our balanced state. This includes moments when the wisest thing to do is just to stay with the feeling and not take any immediate action in the Here-Now.

Anxiety, frustration, and disappointment/sadness inherently hold the information that allows us to stay self-powered. When used effectively, thoughts, which by nature limit and define, are also useful and extraordinarily valuable when we can choose when and how to use them. Thinking has tremendous value and can complement the knowledge gained through direct experience. When, however, in a nanosecond a feeling becomes a feeling-thought, thinking loses its practical value.

Note the difference between thinking about simply leaving on a business trip next Tuesday, and then thinking about leaving on a business trip next Tuesday, which *also* means you will miss your son's birthday.

In this circumstance, to experience sadness at missing your son's birthday is natural. Stay with the feeling of sadness and let it guide you to take some action, such as planning an even more exciting birthday party for when you return.

We have learned to piggyback our feeling of sadness, which is experienced as guilt, then spend our time in the past, distorting ourselves in the negative. In this situation, the negative self-talk may sound like, "I have never given my son enough time. I don't deserve to be a parent."

Guilt consumes energy and prevents us from fully experiencing the present.

Feelings get piggybacked almost instantaneously. We can use this time-space Model to identify which feeling has been piggybacked. We begin by noticing the structure of our thoughts (where we are in time-space). Once we know where we are in time-space, we can shift our attention to the feeling we have piggybacked, experience it, and use it to return to self-powerment.

What does it mean to experience a feeling fully? It means to give our full attention to the bodily experience that is occurring at that moment.

When our emotional need for security has been challenged and we find ourselves in the future, we need to shift our focus and be present with the anxiety that is occurring in the body. We *feel* anxiety in the pit of our stomach. When we recognize we are focusing on other people, situations, or experiences, we need to shift our attention to and be with the feeling of frustration, which is occurring in our body. We *feel* frustration in the tension in the neck area. When our adequacy need has been challenged and we find ourselves in the past, we need to shift attention to and be with the feeling of sadness or disappointment, which is occurring in the body. We *feel* sadness in the space in and around our heart.

When this has become a life habit, any feeling signal that one of our emotional needs is in wobble takes us immediately into our body, where we experience the natural feeling without allowing it to take us out of the Here-Now.

For practical purposes, we have to go to the future to plan; we have to go back to the past to remember. Sometimes we want to think about other people and things, and sometimes we want to look at our own strengths and weaknesses. When we leave the Here-Now by choice, it serves us. Any other time, it becomes the vehicle for discharging feelings. My experience is that, when asked, most people say that they spend most of their time "flying around out there"—not in the Here-Now. It takes an incredible amount of energy to move a feeling onto a thought, energy that could be better used to participate fully in life.

This Is a Model about Choice

If you choose to go to the future to plan, or to the past to remember, or to create other people, situations, or experiences, that's great. When, however, you find yourself in the future, in the past, creating other people or things, or distorting yourself when you really want to be fully present in the Here-Now, you know you have piggybacked a feeling. Feelings are the pathway to Self-Powerment. When used as nature intended, they are the roadmaps that allow us to stay in the Here-Now, where we find our intuition, wisdom, and creativity. When we are in the Here-Now, we have the choice to take action or not, to make a decision or to just wait. Anything we decide is based on true free choice, and the decision is made drawing on the widest possible multisensory database.

Our emotional needs of security, control, adequacy, and the natural feelings that let us know they are in wobble are inside us. And then life happens. For example, we get a rejection letter, we make a mistake, or we get criticized. These experiences evoke feelings. Once an experience evokes feeling, we need to stay with the feeling in order to stay in the Here-Now. If we observe that it has taken us out of the Here-Now, we can then use it to get back to our balanced state.

The situation that evoked the feeling is no longer useful until we can approach it self-powered. We have learned to go in the wrong direction—directing the natural feeling onto a feeling-thought. Now the situation is overloaded and becomes the stage for the play of our personal drama. The true essence of the experience is lost.

The Linchmen

We have discussed how piggybacking our feelings takes us out of the Here-Now. However, we have a desire to return there because it is our place of self-powerment. We are kept out of the Here-Now once we leave it by judgments, comparisons, and negations. *Negation* is used here to indicate that which is not occurring. I call these three—judgments, comparisons, and negations—"Linchmen." The structure of the Linchmen is to pull our focus to the thing being judged, the things being compared, or the things that are not occurring. When we use any of the Linchmen, we shift our focus away from ourselves in the Here-Now, the only place we can fully participate in life. Sometimes, when people are in my seminar, they compare it to others they have taken, instead of being fully present at that time with the material and experiences presented to them. In another instance, when I was on a bus tour in beautiful Bali, I sat beside a woman who talked incessantly about her recent trip to England and missed the present experience. In both these instances, these people are allowing Linchmen to control them.

Essential Principles

In the I Am, we deal with what is; we experience our feelings and use them as nature intended. The natural feelings of anxiety, frustration, and disappointment are indicators whose inherent information allows us to act on our environment to stay secure, in control, and adequate. Feeling-thought structures are the conditioning that keeps us away from our place of Self-Powerment. When we look at them in terms of where they take us in time and space, we can see them clearly and can stop them from occurring.

Three essential principles are illustrated in the Self-Powerment Model:

1. Feelings have a distinct function. Anxiety, frustration, and disappointment are internal indicators that our emotional needs are out of balance, and they give us the information to get back to our balanced state. Other feelings have important functions, as well. Like the feelings we discuss, they have not been allowed free and authentic expression in our culture.

Thought is abstraction, which inherently implies limitation. The whole is too much. There is no way by which thought can get hold of the whole, because thought only abstracts; it limits and defines. And the past from which thought draws contains only a certain limited amount. The present is not contained in thought, thus an analysis cannot cover the moment of analysis.

—David Bohm, *On Dialogue*[1]

Thought takes us out of direct experience. It takes us to the past or the future, and it shifts focus to other people, situations, and experiences. It closes off access to the Here-Now. Thought condenses and thereby limits experience.

It is in the Here-Now that we are mentally silent. This silence makes room for awareness to emerge from our deeper wisdom within.

We have learned to think about almost everything. We think about thoughts, about feelings, about perceptions, and about behavior. It's remarkable that we spend almost our whole waking life thinking. We wake up thinking, we take a shower thinking, we make love thinking, we play golf thinking, we work thinking.

There is no doubt that thinking has an important place in our lives; it is immensely valuable and quite indispensable to a civilized society. But thinking is not life. Life is to be experienced, and, when necessary we can think. We have learned to think all the time and experience occasionally, for example, when a crisis surprises us out of thought. Both Gary Zukav[2] in *The Seat of the Soul* and Eckhart Tolle in *The Power of Now*[3] make this point clearly and powerfully. Often, people need an external crisis to approach the deeper level of reality. This does not have to be the typical way. We can do this by simply being aware of our option to experience life and awareness.

Beyond thinking is the deeper reality of awareness. We don't avoid our situations by not thinking; we open up to a new and more expansive way of experiencing them.

To approach the deeper reality of life is really nothing more than discovering the value of direct experience and the use of feelings to stay self-powered.

2. Inherent in the experience of feelings is the information we need to stay self-powered. Feelings are felt. They are experienced. "Feelings are our most genuine path to knowledge," says Audre Lorde. In the Self-Powerment Model, feelings allow access to focus, control, and competence.[4]

3. These feelings get piggybacked in a nanosecond. Feeling-thoughts are what we have mistakenly come to know as feelings. When we examine these feeling-thoughts, they are always outside of the I Am. They take us to the future, the past, other people and things, or they distort us in the positive or negative. The key to reconnecting to the original feeling is to find out where we are in time and space by observing the structure of our thought. Where we are in time and space tells us what feeling we have piggybacked. We can then experience the feeling, act on our environment, and stay in the Here-Now.

Physicists have used time and space to understand and describe how one object relates to another. In this Self-Powerment Model, time and space are used as references to orient us back to our place of self-powerment. How exciting to use time and space in such a way that ultimately we do not have to use them at all!

It is necessary to identify the structurally learned patterns of our thinking and communication. These patterns hold the information that allows access to direct experience. Where are we in time and space? Are we focusing on others or fragmenting ourselves? Are we judging, comparing, or negating? When we shift our focus to how we structure our thoughts and communication, as opposed to their content, when we shift to *how* from *what* we are thinking and communicating, a degree of detachment occurs. This detachment allows us to determine whether we have made a choice to pay attention to what we are thinking or talking about, or whether we are coming from a structurally learned pattern. It is by observing our thought structures and what takes us out of the Here-Now that we can then detach from them, and choose to return, without thought, to the I Am.

Time and space are our helpmates. Knowing where we are in time (past, present, or future) and where we are in space (energy focused inside ourselves, energy focused on other things and people, or distorting ourselves) enables us to connect to our feelings—feelings we have learned not to feel!

Peter Russell in *Waking Up in Time* tells us,

> *Our consensus trance is not voluntary; it begins at birth, without our conscious agreement. All authority is surrendered to the parents, family members, and other caretakers, who initially are regarded as omniscient and omnipotent. Induction is not limited to short sessions; it involves years of repeated reinforcement. Clinical therapists would consider [it] highly unethical to use force, but our cultural hypnotists often do: a slap on the wrist or a severe reprimand for misbehaving. Or perhaps subtler, but equally powerful, emotional pressures: "I love you only if you think and behave as I tell you." Finally, and most significantly, the conditioning is intended to be permanent. It*

may come from the very best of intentions, but it is, neverthe-
less, meant to have lasting effect on our personalities and on the
way we evaluate the world.[5]

Can you imagine our human conditioning being as thor-
ough as this? The conditioning claims that *what* we think is
reality. Any evidence to the contrary is discounted, and we
continue to maintain our firm conviction that *how* we think
is so.

Thank you to the physicists who brought us an awareness
of time-space that is not charged with content like, "She
never loved me," "They wouldn't let me in the school I
wanted," "If I haven't made VP by now, I never will." Shifting the focus to where thoughts take us in time and space by-
passes all the content and reveals the feeling that, when we
allow ourselves to experience it, brings us back to the Here-
Now, our place of self-powerment. Anyone can do it.

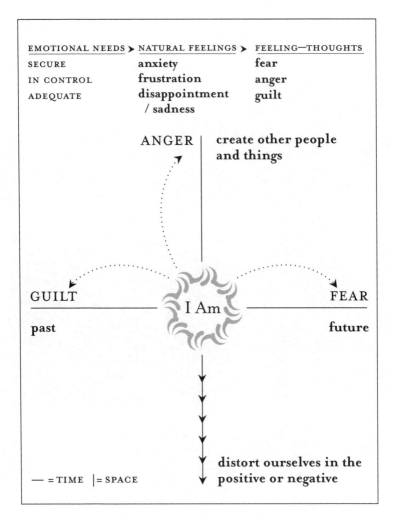

EMOTIONAL NEEDS ➤	NATURAL FEELINGS ➤	FEELING—THOUGHTS
SECURE	anxiety	fear
IN CONTROL	frustration	anger
ADEQUATE	disappointment / sadness	guilt

ANGER | create other people and things

GUILT   I Am   FEAR

past   future

— = TIME | = SPACE

distort ourselves in the positive or negative

Three

SOME TOOLS

Ask Yourself, "Where Am I—Now?"

Referring to the Model on page 57, where do you go on it? Think about where you spend a lot of your time, without choice. Do you go to the future all by yourself? (I'll never get this done.) Do you go to the past and take other people with you? (I would have made VP instead of Peter, if only I had gotten my MBA.) Are you creating or focusing on others (boyfriend, girlfriend, husband, wife, kids, boss, and so forth)? Do you distort yourself in the positive or the negative? ("I'm not smart enough; I don't have enough education; I know this; if they had listened to me, they would have it all done.")

Once you determine where you go in time and space, you can start to listen to *how* you say what you say, rather than just what you say. Most of the time what you say is just a vehicle to piggyback feelings anyway. Listen to the structure of how you create what you say, using the dimensions of time and space (tenses and pronouns).

Conduct a serious observation over a period of time that is doable for you. This can range from a couple of hours to a half-day period. Make at least ten to twenty observations of where you are in time and space, and, referring to Chart A1 on the following page, place a check mark in two of the four columns for each observation.

Chart A1: (Reader's Chart)

FUTURE	PAST	CREATE OTHER PEOPLE & THINGS	DISTORT SELF IN THE POSITIVE OR NEGATIVE

Repeat this task, giving a trusted friend or coworker a copy of Chart A1 and a brief introduction to the Model, and ask them to choose their own time to observe you for half a day, noting where you are in time and space. Discuss the results with them, and solicit their helpful feedback. If you do not have someone conveniently able to help, you can just record your own place in time and space and wait a day or so to look at your recordings. Often it is easier to see more objectively after some time has passed.

Chart A2: (Reviewer's Chart)

FUTURE	PAST	CREATE OTHER PEOPLE & THINGS	DISTORT SELF IN THE POSITIVE OR NEGATIVE

If you are like most of us, you have determined that you go all over the chart—into the future and the past, creating other people and things, and distorting yourself in the positive or negative without choice. Did you also find that, like most of us, you, too, have a favorite place you tend to go to most often? Let me tell you mine. It's 7:30 A.M., and I will be teaching a seminar at 9:00 A.M. It begins when I'm drying my hair.

"Oh, they're going to hate it. It's the only thing I know how to do for a living. They're going to foreclose on my house, take my children away. I'll be a bag lady in New York City and sleep under the Brooklyn Bridge."

I ask myself, "Where am I?" I'm in the future. What am I really feeling? I'm anxious. I want to do a good job in the seminar. However, instead of feeling my anxiety, I piggyback it onto a thought and it takes me into the future. So, I feel my anxiety, come back to the present, and use the anxiety to focus on the present. I come back to drying my hair, experience the moment, and I am ready to deal with the seminar when I am in the seminar. When I am focused in the present with my intuitive experience of who I am, I see clearly. I have everything I need in the present to do the best work I can possibly do. I stay with my focus on fully participating in the experience that I am in now. Referring again to the Self-Powerment Model on page 57, put a check mark on the chart where you find your "favorite" place that you go to without choice. It needs to exist in a quadrant or directly on one of the time-space axes. Identify your story (personal drama) that takes you there. Write it down on the following page, and note how many times in the next few weeks you return exactly to this "favorite place" without choice.

MY STORY that takes me to my "favorite" place without choice.

What Is Your Favorite Linchman?

We know now that it is the piggybacking of natural feelings onto thought that takes us out of the Here-Now. Since we all want to be in the Here-Now, what keeps us out? As discussed, it is the Linchmen—judgments, comparisons, and negations.

The Linchmen are learned thought patterns, which keep us from our place of self-powerment. In Chart B1, there are three columns marked Judgments, Comparisons, and Negations. Seriously observe your conversations for one half-day. If one half-day is not doable, at least focus for a couple of hours on your Linchmen. Note any time you use a Linchman, and put a check mark in the appropriate column. From your observations, did you discover one you use most frequently? The next step is to repeat this task with a trusted friend or coworker, asking him or her to note your use of the Linchmen over a half-day period (or whatever time period is doable). Again, give the person a brief introduction to this Self-Powerment Model and a copy of Chart B2. Discuss the results, and solicit their helpful feedback.

Chart B1: (Reader's Chart)

JUDGMENTS	COMPARISONS	NEGATIONS

Chart B2: (Reviewer's Chart)

JUDGMENTS	COMPARISONS	NEGATIONS

Create Your Personal Space

To see clearly, it is often important that we detach from the situation in which we find ourselves in order to view it from a fresh perspective. We need to do this frequently because the learned thought patterns are strong and have intense momentum. The following practice enables you to break free and come back to the Here-Now.

Close your eyes and take a deep breath in. Breathe it out. Do this three times, each time allowing yourself to let go of any tension. Now create a place for yourself where you feel secure, in control, and adequate. Choose a place in nature or indoors. It can have a lot of detail or very little, a lot of color or very little. The only essential ingredient is that here you feel secure, in control, and adequate. It is a place where you know everything and everything knows you. This is your own personal space. It belongs to you and only you.

For the first week of your practice, go to your personal space at least five times a day. Once you become familiar with this practice and experience the benefits of its use, integrate it into your daily life, using it especially when you are in wobble.

This practice takes almost no time and costs nothing. It brings you back to being grounded and centered, back to the Here-Now. You will likely find that you feel a certain calm when grounded and centered, and that this feeling becomes more familiar and enjoyable as you continue to revisit this special personal space.

The choice to go to this personal space can be one of your most valuable ways to refocus your attention and bring yourself back into the Here-Now.

The Importance of the Journey to Ithaca

We have learned to be so goal-oriented that we actually believe it is acceptable to focus a tremendous amount of our time, energy, and resources to thinking about our goals. In other words, we feel it is worthwhile to spend a great deal of time in the future. We are measured and judged by our achievement of goals. When we finally reach our goals, we know how long the satisfaction lasts. In "Ithaca," the Greek poet C. R. Cavafy challenges us to reconsider this learned focus on goals.

When you start on your journey to Ithaca
Then pray that the road is long
Full of adventure, full of knowledge
Do not fear the Lestrygonians
and the angry Cyclops and the angry Poseidon
You will never meet such as these on your path
If your thoughts remain lofty
If a fine emotion touches your body and your spirit
You will never meet the Lestrygonians
the Cyclops and the fierce Poseidon
if you do not carry them within your soul,
if your soul does not raise them up before you.

Then pray that the road is long
That the summer mornings are many
That you will enter parts seen for the first time
with pleasure, with such joy!
Stop at Phoenician markets and purchase fine merchandise
Mother-of-Pearl and corals, amber and ebony
and pleasurable perfumes of all kinds.
Buy as many pleasurable perfumes as you can,
Visit hosts of Egyptian cities
to learn and learn from those who have knowledge.

Always keep Ithaca fixed in your mind
To arrive there is your ultimate goal
But do not hurry the voyage at all
It is better to let it last for long years,
and even to anchor at the isle when you are old
rich with all that you have gained on the way
not expecting that Ithaca will offer you riches.

Ithaca has given you the beautiful voyage
without her you would have never taken the road
But she has nothing more to give you.
And if you find her poor, Ithaca has not defrauded you
With the great wisdom you have gained

With so much experience
You must surely have understood by then what Ithaca
    means.

This poem strongly suggests that the only reason to create a goal is to get the wisdom and learnings gathered along the way to attaining it.

It is better to let it last for long years,
and even to anchor at the isle when you are old
rich with all that you have gained on the way
not expecting that Ithaca will offer you riches.

Ithaca has given you the beautiful voyage
without her you would have never taken the road[6]

Since life is always Here-Now, that is where we find the wisdom of life. We can choose to make optimum use of the Here-Now in order to gain the wisdom it holds. **The only reason to create the goal is to learn from the journey.** It is the goal that allows the journey to begin. It is the starting point. It is the experiences along the way that create the path to wisdom.

The traditional way of goal setting is to be at A and to set goal Z. Then we do task B and we siphon—that is draw off or empty—a little bit of B to see if we are on target with Z. We do the same thing with C, that is, we siphon off a little of C to see if we are on target with Z. We continue until we reach our goal, and with a high degree of probability, we will attain something near to it. We evaluate (compare and judge) every experience on whether it is moving us toward goal Z. If the data from the experience do not fit with goal Z, we minimize or discount those data as not valuable. In effect, by doing this, we eliminate the consideration of all but one or several of the many possibilities.

Note how this applies to the example of a consultant who hired an assistant to help him complete a project. The next week he met someone eminently more qualified for the project; however, because he had already hired someone, he did not even consider hiring the more qualified person.

In the traditional way of goal setting, we take each experience and evaluate it solely on the basis of whether or not it is going to get us to Z, as defined at point A.

I present this concept visually as follows:

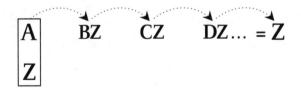

We have learned to believe that if we think of the goal, plan strategies, and create an overall game plan, which we follow precisely, then we will get to Z.

A goal, like any thought or concept, is limiting. I suggest a new way of goal setting. Set goal Z, then fully live A, B, C, and D—which may alter the overall game plan. Fully experience each step along the journey, and integrate and utilize the learnings from them. As we begin to actualize the plan, the reality of what we experience along the way can lead to many different outcomes. These unique outcomes from the experiences along the way are our compass pointing to the achievement of the most beneficial goal. We don't change the goal, per se; we just open to greater possibilities to enhance it. When it is wise to change the goal, the learnings from the experiences make that evident.

In this second approach, there is a new value and emphasis placed on creating possibilities from each experience as well as on the achievement of the goal. I represent this visually in the following diagram. There is reward for surprise.

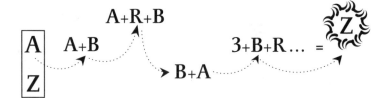

Four

LET'S GET PRACTICAL

Having a tool is valuable only if we learn how to use it. So, how do we learn to listen differently? How do we learn to listen to the structure of thoughts and communication, rather than just to their content?

Did you ever study a foreign language in school? When a teacher began to lecture about declining pronouns or to teach us about past participles, the pluperfect, and future conditional tenses, that's when I cut class and went across the street for a slice of pizza and an orange soda. If the teacher had explained that tenses orient me in time and pronouns orient me in space, and had pointed out the benefits of knowing this, I may have stayed. So too, if I had been told that when I was worrying about my boyfriend's fidelity, I was really feeling frustrated at not being able to control that situation, I would have learned something valuable. When we listen for tenses and pronouns, we begin to hear where we are in time and space.

We can use our orientation in time and space to identify what feeling we have piggybacked and can use that information to reconnect to the feeling, experience it, and use it to get back to the Here-Now.

Let's Practice

Referring again to the Self-Powerment Model on page 80, you can see once you have identified where you are in time and space, there are two arrows that point down.

The top arrow indicates what the feeling-thought is. The bottom arrow indicates what the natural feeling is. To deepen our understanding of how the Model works, let's practice with some sentence structures.

Here is a sentence that we hear often at work: "You should have gotten it to me last week."

Here is a sentence that we hear often in relationships: "You should have asked for my opinion before you made that decision."

Referring to the Model, where is *you?* It is on the space line axis of creating other people and things. Now, what is the feeling-thought? It is anger. And what is the feeling? Frustration!

Regarding *should have,* where is this on the Model? It is on the time line axis in the past. The feeling-thought is guilt, and the feeling is disappointment or sadness.

Thus, the way to experience "You should have gotten it to me last week" or "You should have called last night" in the Here-Now is to feel your frustration and disappointment.

EMOTIONAL ➤	NATURAL ➤	FEELING—	SAMPLE
NEEDS	FEELINGS	THOUGHTS	SITUATIONS
SECURE	**anxiety**	**fear**	**rejections**
IN CONTROL	**frustration**	**anger**	**mistakes**
ADEQUATE	**disappointment**	**guilt**	**criticisms**
	/ sadness		

**create other people
and things**
∨
ANGER
distorted feeling / thought
∨
frustration
natural feeling

――――――――――― I Am ―――――――――――

past   **future**
∨   ∨
GUILT   FEAR
distorted feeling / thought   distorted feeling / thought
∨   ∨
disappointment   **anxiety**
natural feeling   natural feeling

— = TIME | = SPACE

**distort ourselves in the
positive or negative**

Here are two more examples. "I am not going to be able to lose that weight—never," and "I can't get this done by Thursday." *Never* and *can't* are negations. They are one of the three Linchmen. It does not exist in the I Am. *By Thursday* and *never* take us on the time axis to the future. The feeling-thought is fear. The feeling is anxiety. The way to experience "I can't get it done by Thursday" or "I am not going to lose weight—never," in the Here-Now is to feel your anxiety.

When we piggyback a feeling onto a thought, the content of the communication becomes the focus, taking us away from the feeling evoked in the Here-Now.

Let's try two more examples: "I would have received the raise if I had worked harder," and "My girlfriend wouldn't have broken up with me if I had tried harder to be a good boyfriend." As used in both examples, where is *would have?* It is on the time axis in the past. The feeling-thought is guilt, and the feeling is disappointment or sadness. The Linchman comparison is seen in *worked harder* and *tried harder*. So the grounded and centered way to experience this sentence is simply to feel your disappointment.

Let's now elaborate on the situation in which Rachel invites her boyfriend over for the evening. He's late and then very late. We've all been in this type of situation; just change the names and address. Rachel's boyfriend is Tom, and because

Rachel is not accustomed yet to observing her thoughts, we will add her good friend Connie, who will do this for her.

RACHEL:

It's already eight-fifteen. Tom was supposed to be here at eight o'clock. He's always late. Why can't he be on time for once?

CONNIE:

Come on, Rachel, you really can't say **always***. I know you are anxious about whether he is coming or not.*

RACHEL:

Okay then, "sometimes." If he's not here soon, the steak will get dry and the vegetables will be overcooked.

CONNIE:

You're focused on the dinner. I know you are frustrated that he's not here already. Let's call him at home to at least see if he's left. If he's not there, we can try his cell.

[*Rachel makes the two telephone calls, but there is no answer.*]

RACHEL:

Connie, it's eight-thirty. Now I'm really getting upset. The dinner is ruined for sure.

CONNIE:

I know you're disappointed that he's not here by now. You're really a great cook. It's disappointing to have worked so hard to prepare him a nice meal and not have him here to enjoy it.

Hey, this is a good time to look at that batch of pictures of the two of you that you just picked up.

RACHEL:

I hate him. I need to find another boyfriend. He's so insensitive to who I am and what I need.

CONNIE:

Look, Rachel, I know you are really frustrated and probably feeling out of control now. Remember our lunch last week when you were telling me about all the wonderful things he has done for you lately? Let's keep this in perspective.

RACHEL:

If I marry him, what if he's late all the time? That will drive me crazy, Connie.

CONNIE:

Hey, you're way into the future now, talking of some possibility.

RACHEL:

Connie, now it's nine. What if something happened to him? What if he got into a car accident? He could be hurt somewhere.

CONNIE:

I know you're feeling anxious, Rachel. Try his cell one more time, also his sister. She may have an explanation.

RACHEL:

No, I'm tired of playing detective here. I hate him. I don't care if he's dead.

CONNIE:

Slow down, Rachel. That's serious judgment stuff. Let's wait and see what the reason is for his being late.

[*Rachel is adamant.*]

RACHEL:

I just know that he's met another woman. She's probably

younger and more beautiful than I am. I bet he's with her right now.

CONNIE:

Now you're back to being anxious and frustrated again. Chances are there's a perfectly reasonable explanation.

[*It's 9:45 P.M. Rachel's fears have completely taken over at this stage.*]

RACHEL:

Oh, my God. I'll never get married and have children. How will I be able to deal with the loneliness?

CONNIE:

I know you must be feeling insecure now. Please try not to take it personally. All we know is that Tom is late.

[*At 10:00, the doorbell rings. Rachel runs to the door and flings it open. There is Tom, breathless and covered with mud.*]

TOM:

You'll never believe what happened. As I was coming into the city, I took what I thought would be a shortcut because I didn't want to be late. Well, I got a flat tire on a country road. I forgot to recharge the battery on my cell this morning and had to wait an hour before somebody came along to give me a ride. A great guy. He was even nice enough to drive me right here. With all that rain and mud, I must look a mess. I'm so sorry, honey.

Now, let's move from the home front to the workplace so we can see how flexible this Model is in application. Here is a challenging conversation between a manager and her employee. This conversation is written verbatim. As you read, try to identify where the manager and employee are in time and space and determine what the feeling-thoughts are as well as the corresponding feeling for each.

Employee/Manager Interaction

EMPLOYEE:

I'm very frustrated that not everyone is taking this project seriously. It's an insult to management that when we ask for something to be done, it doesn't get done. I admit some people are doing more than their share of the work, but these few can't pull most of the load. I'm afraid I'll never be able to get anything done if you don't make these people listen to me and make them do the work. I don't know if they're lazy or just can't organize their time or if they're not team players, but it's the same people all the time.

[*Here's a well-meaning and sound human resource response from the manager.*]

MANAGER:

Let's look at this project that you're trying to get done in the total context of what they're doing. I know that some people have different work pressures than others. People have different field sizes; we have given them different assignments. What I'm hearing from the team leaders is that there's nobody out there sitting on their hands waiting for their next assignment. They're all pressured with multiple priorities, and what I suggest is that you ask some of the people who have not been able to get this project done what their plan is. Have the team leaders call them in and say, "You seem to be struggling with getting this project done, and we wanted to have it done by the end of the year; it doesn't look like that's going to happen for you. What's your plan? When do you think you might be able to get it done? And how can I support you in that?"

Now, let's look at what this dialogue sounds like when the manager is a practitioner of the Self-Powerment Model and focuses on staying in the present moment and grounding and centering her employee. It represents a whole new way of communicating.

EMPLOYEE:

I'm very frustrated that not everyone is taking this project seriously. It's an insult to management that when we ask for something to be done, it doesn't get done. Some people do more than their share of the work. I'm afraid I'll never be able to get anything done if you don't make these people listen to me and make them do the work. I don't know if they're lazy or just can't organize their time or if they're not team players, but it's the same people all the time.

MANAGER:

Chris, you say you're feeling frustrated. Talk to me about that.

[*Note how the manager focuses Chris on her feeling of frustration, centering her back on herself.*]

EMPLOYEE:

I'm totally— I feel overwhelmed with frustration—it's just— I can't get anything done. No one helps me; no one is doing their job. I give them directives, Betsey, but they don't follow up.

MANAGER:

So, sounds like you're out of control.

[*The manager labels the emotional need for Chris (out of control), again centering her back to herself.*]

EMPLOYEE:

Totally.

MANAGER:

What can I do to help you with this?

EMPLOYEE:

You have to talk to them, make them listen to me.

MANAGER:

Rather than talk to them, how can I help you?

[*Once again, the manager takes Chris back to the Here-Now with the focus being on Chris.*]

EMPLOYEE:

I have no idea. I don't know.

MANAGER:

Yes, you do. Focus on you—not on them. You're very capable, Chris. You can do this.

[*The manager gives Chris the acknowledgment that she is in control and capable of identifying solutions.*]

EMPLOYEE:

Well, they could've held a meeting last Monday to discuss the project, but they just didn't do it. They could've gotten together for a coffee break in the afternoon and discussed it after I had a meeting with a few of them.

MANAGER:

Look, those possibilities don't exist anymore—they're in the past. It's pretty disappointing and frustrating when projects don't go well—let's look at what's happening now—and what we can do now—to get these people going.

[*The Manager listens to the structure of communication and identifies that Chris is in the past (could have), is focused on other people, and identifies Chris's feelings of disappointment and frustration.*]

EMPLOYEE:

But, Betsey, you don't understand. We'll never meet the deadline. They're never going to get it done. Every time we have a discussion about what has to be done, they don't listen, they don't follow up—especially John; he's just totally ridiculous.

MANAGER:

Listen, you're way out there—way into the future. What's going on now? It sounds like you're frustrated and anxious about doing a good job.

[*The manager, still observing the structure of Chris's communi-cation, identifies that she is in the future (never) and is still* focused on other people and things (John, they) and acknowledges Chris's feelings of frustration and anxiety.]

EMPLOYEE:

You know, you're right. I really am feeling anxious about how you're going to view me and my job and everyone else, as a matter of fact. I just— I don't want anyone to think I'm not capable.

MANAGER:

Hey! It's really okay. Let's work together to look at what you can do with your resources right now. Once you've identified this, let me know if I can help you somehow.

This dialogue illustrates how we can use personal choice and deliberation to help ground and center individuals in the Here-Now. We can help them see that they can choose where they are in time and space and the benefits of choosing to be in the Here-Now.

When they are in the future, they have piggybacked anxiety and can use that anxiety to focus on getting the task done. When they are creating other people and things, they have piggybacked frustration and can use the frustration to get back in control so that energy is available to them to deal with the current reality. When they are in the past, they have piggybacked sadness/disappointment and can use the sadness to experience closure and come back to the present, feeling adequate to get the task done.

To help deepen this understanding, take one of your written communications, such as a personal letter or work memorandum of at least one to two pages. Referring to Chart C, analyze your writing, noting with a check mark where you are for each statement. Then, rewrite your document in the present tense. Note the difference when you exercise personal choice regarding where you position yourself in time and space. If you do not have something to use on hand, go ahead and write down a letter to a friend, partner, or coworker describing an issue you have. You do not have to send it; rather, it can be used for this exercise and help you examine your own language.

Chart C: (Reader's Chart)

FUTURE	PAST	CREATE OTHER PEOPLE & THINGS	DISTORT SELF IN THE POSITIVE OR NEGATIVE

In his book *The Dancing Wu Li Masters*, Gary Zukav quotes David Finkelstein, a professor of physics, who writes,

> *Symbols (language) do not follow the same rules as experience. . . . In short the problem is not in the language, the problem is the language.*[7]

The problem is, indeed, the language, when we view it in terms of a lack of awareness of how we structure its content. When language **is** used as a tool structurally to orient us to the Here-Now, it becomes the vehicle to connect us to feelings, which are the pathway to self-powerment.

How we structure what we say, and not what we say, becomes the crucial element in communication. Does our communication keep us focused in the Here-Now—in the I Am? Does it contain dialogue in which what you say is the stimulus for my response, and my response is the stimulus for what you say, instead of what I say being created by what I think?

When we begin to hear the feelings embedded in the content and can discern them, we can use these feelings as nature intended—to keep us grounded and centered.

Five

ANY QUESTIONS?

Many people who have taken my seminar, and others who have just heard about it, have questions they want answered. Here are some of the most frequently asked questions and my answers. The questions are written verbatim.

Q: *When you are in the I Am, aren't you self-centered, impulsive, and caring only about yourself?*

A: No. When you live in the I Am, you know intuitively that you are connected to everyone. Actually, your entire experience of self changes dramatically. It is here that you can detach from the personal image of yourself and experience the universal energy, which integrates all of us. In the Here-Now, impulsiveness does not exist because the experience of the centered present is all that there is. The connectedness of experience is found in the I Am. To care only about yourself involves separation from others.

Q: *How can you be in the I Am in the workplace, which is so goal-oriented?*

A: In the I Am, you understand that the only reason to create a goal is to get the wisdoms and learnings from the experience. Once an organization realizes that supporting the people who work there to come into the Here-Now allows them to utilize productively the learnings from their hands-on experience, the organization will refocus on creating possibilities as a critical step to increasing profitability. Create possibilities, and profitability follows.

Q: *How can I remember to stay in the I Am?*

A: In this Model, remembering means unlearning the patterns that keep you out of the I Am. Since there are countless content patterns, it makes much more sense to reposition yourself using time and space. Vigilant attention to where you are in time and space allows you to refocus your energy onto your feelings and use them to stay self-powered. Checking in with yourself frequently every day, asking the question, "Where am I?" is a great way to start.

Q: *How can I get others who aren't in the I Am to go there?*

A: The most practical way is to be there yourself. When you are grounded and centered in the Here-Now, others experience you very differently. On a practical level, start to ask different kinds of questions, like "Where are you?" or "How many people are here with us?" Ask if people are aware of where they are in time and space. The significance of observing and labeling the structure of your dialogue and of communicating about feelings are meaningful topics for conversation.

Q: *I don't believe it works.*

A: Don't believe me yet. Try it for yourself. Let your experience provide your own evidence. Try it for a few weeks, and notice if there is any change in your experience of yourself, your relationships, and your environment. As with any new tool, you have to practice and get the experience while practicing to really see how it works. What better tool to develop an expertise with than a tool that allows you to stay self-powered?

Q: *If I am in the I Am, I'll probably just want to have fun and live for today.*

A: When you live in the I Am, you know that each day is a precious gift to experience and from which to learn. When you are in the I Am, you're connected to the eternal present and the vastness of your internal universe. Life becomes something for which you are deeply grateful.

Q: *How can I stay in the I Am when life dictates that I must think ahead to be prepared for the unexpected?*

A: When you live in the I Am, full participation in your experience allows you most of the information needed to deal with the unexpected. That full participation in the moment prepares you for the unexpected. For example, a woman I know needed to sell her house but had nowhere to go to live. Once she put up the "for sale" sign and started to manifest the experience of selling her house by talking about it with others, a wonderful, surprising opportunity opened up that was helpful not only to her but also to a friend as well as the children of both families.

Q: *If I'm in the I Am in a relationship or work environment and a partner or a coworker who has taken your seminar on living in the Here-Now isn't, what can I say to get them back?*

A: The key question for helping someone to become aware of where they are in time and space is, "Where are you—now?" It is essential to shift from a focus on the content of the communication to where that content is taking you in time and space. Re-referencing yourself or others allows an altered perspective, which then helps the individual to get grounded and centered, and back to the present moment where energy is focused inside ourselves.

Q: *When do you see yourself beyond the I Am?*

A: When you're in the I Am, there is no beyond. There is an entirely unique relationship to the present because you know that that is all there is. You respect and honor your day because that day is the gift of living.

Q: *When using the I Am process in coaching and development, how can we clearly set expectations?*

A: The key expectation is that people participate fully in their experience. This framework allows all individuals to experience self-powerment, which includes accountability, responsibility, and integrity as intrinsic elements of how they relate in their lives. Expectations that are set for the future, without choice, take our energy from the present. Choosing both to create an expectation and to participate fully in every experience allows a whole new approach for utilizing expectations as the means of ongoing learning.

Q: *Do you need a certain requirement to teach this to others?*

A: The only requirement to teach being in the Here-Now is to be grounded and centered in your own life, with vigilant attention to where you are in time and space. Being a role model for living in the present, with energy focused inside yourself, using feelings as nature intended—as the pathway to self-powerment—is the most effective tool available to you. When you are in the Here-Now, you automatically invite others to join you there. When you are in the Here-Now, you can't help but be a teacher of present-moment living.

Q: *How can I manage work and family and have time for me?*

A: When you are in the I Am, you have more than enough time and energy to address what life presents to you. You aren't dissipating your energy by worrying about the future or regretting and reworking something in the past. You aren't giving your power away to other people and events. You are focusing on the priorities that enable you to feel secure, in control, and adequate. When you use your energy to accomplish the task at hand, predictably you accomplish it with efficiency and creativity.

Remember, you must take care of yourself first. This isn't selfish but healthy self-care. Then you still have more than enough time and energy to give to others—and you will give it cleanly, without the negative charge of resentment.

Q: *So often people come to me looking for answers, and since there are infinite possibilities, how can I help them to see* *they already have the solution and that my feedback is just one possibility?*

A: By not giving an answer, you insist that people look within themselves for the answer. When you give an answer, it is your definition of reality that they are buying. Let people discover the answer themselves, by helping them to re-reference themselves to the place where the answer becomes known through their own resources.

Q: *What will happen when we are all capable of remaining in the I Am?*

A: When we move to the next level of consciousness, where people's primary motivation is to be of service, and where people feel self-powered to behave in ways that are inspired by their intuition as well as by reason, we can focus on addressing problems as paradoxes with the movement toward the right relationship with what is. How that manifests is totally unknown and is a wonderful muse as we create possibilities.

Q: *What about the search for new beginnings?*

A: "Always keep Ithaca fixed in your mind/To arrive there is your ultimate goal/But do not hurry the voyage at all. . . ." New beginnings become the nature of what is so. Creating new possibilities becomes the focus when you are grounded and centered. New beginnings are new possibilities come into being. They are one and the same.

Q: *How do you deal with someone who is consistently negative when you're trying to be in the I Am?*

A: When people are being negative, they are saying what isn't—not what is. You can help them by encouraging them to refocus on what is so. Help them deal with what is so, rather than create the negative. It is highly probable that they have piggybacked a feeling and have discharged all their energy, so your gift is to refocus them onto the place where they can acknowledge and use their feelings to get back to being self-powered. Just keep asking, "What is so?" When you have compassion, you respond with concern and caring, rather than reacting and becoming defensive.

Q: *How do I apply the principle to an individual who is passive-aggressive and does not acknowledge any feelings or actions?*

A: Clearly that person is feeling frustrated and out of control. They are also feeling a tremendous amount of anxiety that they have piggybacked onto behavior. Labeling their feelings is a good way to begin. Remember, when people are self-powered, they relate to others with respect. When emotional needs are in wobble, they must be addressed and that person is only trying, albeit unsuccessfully, to experience security and control in their life. Speak to those emotional concerns.

Q: *How can you take principles of I Am to upwardly change the organization from a top-down to a bottom-up one?*

A: When you are in the I Am, you have more than enough time and energy. You are connected to the place of accountability, responsibility, and integrity. As you live from this place, your relationship to your job, your performance, and your team changes dramatically. You role-model the new behaviors and by this influence your coworkers and leaders. There is an increase in passion and productivity, which is clearly demonstrable in the bottom line. Everyone becomes accountable for creating profitability, but not necessarily by rigidly adhering to the procedures and methods created in the old paradigm.

Q: *Is the I Am the only solution to all our daily problems?*

A: There are many ways to deal with daily problems. Grounding and centering oneself in the Here-Now is one of the most practical since it doesn't cost any money or take extra time. All it requires is that we open our awareness to where we are in time and space so we can access and use feelings as nature intended. Grounding and centering allow us to connect to the gateway through which creative solutions become possible. In the I Am, we can see that perhaps we're asking the wrong questions, that something we thought was a problem really isn't, or that a problem itself can be restructured to be seen as an opportunity.

Q: *As society moves at an ever-increasing pace, will it be possible to live in the I Am all the time?*

A: Actually it is essential to be in the Here-Now as the pace of society is increasing. In the Here-Now, there are infinite possibilities at any given moment, which allow for change to be experienced as natural. Since change is, the I Am is the state where change exists and occurs most naturally.

Q: *How can I use the I Am tool at home when I have a wife or husband who always reminds me of the future?*

A: People who live in the future are people who have learned to piggyback their feelings of anxiety. By using anxiety naturally to focus and participate fully in life, a person continually creates the experiences necessary to take care of the future. You can help your wife by assisting her to refocus on the Here-Now. Ask her, "What is happening—now?" Help her to connect with her present-moment feeling and support her in taking the time now to act to feel secure.

Q: *If everything is relative, how do you know what is the real truth?*

A: The real truth exists in this moment. It is the eternal present that provides us with the information that is needed to know what is so.

Q: *How can you just disregard the past if all that you know is learned through experience?*

A: When you fully participate in an experience, you take the wisdom and lessons learned from that experience and incorporate them into your knowing of what is so. It is the integration of the knowing, rather than the content, that provides the wisdom from experience. The learning takes place through the experience, not because of it.

Q: *How do you respond to a child's anxiety such as is expressed in, "I'm really nervous about the test tomorrow?"*

A: Allow the child to experience the anxiety. Talk about it, draw it, dance it, paint it. Anxiety is the feeling that allows the child to focus and be fully in the experience. Of course, knowing the test material is essential. The ability to be clear and focused allows that knowledge to be turned into a successful outcome.

Q: *How can I bring my thoughts back to the Here-Now when I'm already deep in fear?*

A: One way is ask someone for help. Other people are a key resource when you are not grounded and centered. Let them listen, and allow them to identify where you are, and label your feeling. You can then shift your focus to experience the feeling and use it to get back to your natural emotional state of security. Another way is to begin a journal. Just put your pencil on the paper and write. What your internal universe says is a key to getting back to feeling emotionally secure.

Q: *Why don't you talk to our manager to give us some time each day to practice being grounded and centered?*

A: When you have the discipline to take the time each day to get grounded and centered and experience how much more efficient, productive, and creative you are, you will know that it is something you must do, just like eating or drinking. It is not up to the manager to give you the time in which to do it. It is your life and your choice to live self-powered.

Q: *How can you remain in the I Am in traffic?*

A: When you're in traffic, you're in traffic, and that is what is so. Most people want to be somewhere else: in the future, and out of the traffic. They dissipate their energy by leaving the present. But you can choose to take this time, this present moment, to listen to music, muse on possibilities, admire nature, or enjoy being with yourself. It is a time the universe has given you to have for yourself to participate in your life in a way that keeps you self-powered.

Q: *How long does it usually take to realize that you're not in the Here-Now?*

A: Awareness is required, and practice is the key that opens the gateway to self-powerment. The more you practice, the more the awareness of where you are in time and space becomes integrated with how you live your life. Once you are in the I Am, feelings can again be natural indicators to stay grounded and centered.

Q: *How can the person in the I Am help his or her partner stay out of the past?*

A: When a person is in the past without choice it is because they have piggybacked the feeling of sadness/disappointment onto a thought. Identify where the person is in time and what feeling has been piggybacked. Create opportunities for that person to experience their adequacy in the present.

Q: *How do you get into the I Am when a past experience you thought you put closure to shows up again and again?*

A: In his book *The Seat of the Soul,* Gary Zukav[8] says that we are in the earth's school and that the universe is quite compassionate, giving us repeated experiences until the lesson has been learned. The notion is that maybe there are still many learnings that will help you obtain the wisdom you need. Be grateful for the opportunity to learn and grow. We need to participate fully in our experiences, not judge whether they are the "right" ones for us to have.

Actually, we can say that we repeat as a current experience the automatic connection of the feeling to the thought. We are not aware of this connection. When we truly become clear about how we feel and can consciously connect the feeling to the repetitious thought, the nonreality of the thought content becomes apparent.

Q: *I thought that we were supposed to share our feelings.*

A: Feelings are natural indicators to let us know if our emotional needs are in wobble and that we must act on our environment to stay grounded and centered. They are yours to use to stay self-powered. They are internal and individual, and it is a matter of choice whether you share them or not. They are the pathway to self-powerment, the pathway to connect to the soul.

There are many more questions, and I can guarantee that answers evolve at the same rate as our consciousness evolves to receive them.

Six

HERE-NOW AND
THE BOTTOM LINE:
A Look at the Self-Powerment Model
in the Workplace

The Self-Powerment Model is applicable to so very many areas: conflict resolution, effective communication skills, stress management, parenting skills, creative problem-solving, personal coaching, and many more. In this chapter, the business arena is discussed as one example of its many applications.

These times of growing uncertainty and escalated change bring both higher risk and demand for peak performance. To survive and adapt in the business arena, we need to do something different. Einstein told us that we couldn't solve problems at the same level on which they were created.[9]

Now is the time to move to the next generation of business effectiveness. This involves seeing our world and ourselves differently. There is clear evidence from the hard sciences of physics, biology, and neurology, as well as evidence from the fields of psychology, linguistics, and organizational development that confirms that we utilize only a small portion of our innate intelligence and creativity.

> *The intellectual assets of most companies are probably worth at least three or four times the company's tangible book value, yet no CEO I know could honestly claim to be actually utilizing more than 20 percent of his or her firm's intellectual capital base. Can you imagine the fate of any CEO who could only manage 20 percent utilization rate in his or her production capacity, inventory efficiency or any other traditional index of performance? It doesn't even bear thinking about. Yet in this, the most important wealth creating area of all, a 20 percent efficiency rate is considered normal, inevitable, and acceptable. Well, it isn't.*
>
> —Matthew J. Kiernan, *The Eleven Commandments of 21st Century Management*[10]

Why do we use only a fraction of our intellectual capital? Because we think we already know most of what there is to know. We are like the proverbial blind man touching the leg of an elephant and believing it to be a tree trunk.

Until now, innate intelligence and creativity have been grossly underutilized, mainly because of the insistence on quantitative measurement and rewards based solely on direct financial results.

To access this innate intelligence and creativity, which enhance the bottom line, we must expand our vision to see beyond the limitation of what can be measured quantitatively. We must open ourselves more fully to information that is qualitatively valuable. When we do not limit ourselves to concepts or even thought, we become receptive to the multidimensional sensory experience in which intelligence and creativity reside. This information is in the Here-Now and is open to all employees.

To reiterate, there are two quite distinct databases—one from thought and one from direct experience. We have come to believe that thinking is the most powerful source of information for strategic planning, marketing, sales, and other business activities. Indeed, we have been taught to think about everything. In this information age, we believe quantity and organization of information that is compiled through discussion and strategic planning to be the highest form of possibility for innovation and successful outcome. The data that are experienced from thought, however, only continue to add more quantity to existing structures, to remold them or recombine them to try to create innovative change.

We need to include information from the Here-Now. In the Here-Now, time can expand, collapse, curve, and so forth. Space is full or empty, can leap across continents or contain a universe in a grain of sand. Knowing this, consider the possibilities of what can be when we break away from the notions of time and space as absolute. When we let time and space blend into a unified time-space, we discover the boundless creative possibilities of multidimensional experience within each employee.

How does this link with the Self-Powerment Model? Strict focus on the goal, and the gathering of only quantitative evidence to verify achievement minimize the value and learnings found within each experience. To miss the importance of and opportunities to learn from each experience is to reduce significantly the creation of possibilities for enhanced goal achievement. The next step is evident. Drop rigid adherence to the goal, and the creation of possibilities becomes the natural experience. Each experience along the way opens to new possibilities that are cumulative and exponential, and when acted upon, improve results. Living in the Here-Now is the mechanism to achieve this vital expansion.

Consider the following benefits of practicing this new way of being in the workplace.

Employees have more energy. When employees are in the Here-Now, not regretting things that are past and worrying about the future, or shifting their focus outside themselves to others and things, their energy is focused in the present. Since they are no longer using their energy to put feelings onto thoughts—and this happens in most instances all day long—this energy is now available to direct to the task at hand.

Employees are clear and focused on their work in the now. When employees feel secure, in control, and adequate, they use feelings naturally to maintain clarity and focus. Feelings are the tools that nature gives us so that we can maintain balance, clarity, and focus. Feelings contain tremendous information and energy which can be accessed for productive and healthy purposes.

Employees are resilient to change. On the whole, organizations have done remarkably well in adapting to technological changes. What is required now is for employees to experience this same adaptability in their lives.

When we are in the Here-Now, we experience infinite possibilities, which give us greater resources to be resilient to change. We are not trying to hold on to the past and cling to former ways and traditions, nor are we spending energy worrying about the future or projecting. Instead, we are comfortable with what is happening in the moment.

Employees have more productive relationships. When employees no longer create judgments, comparisons, and negations and live in the Here-Now, they are able to interact in a way that allows a new level of combined intelligence. This has never occurred before on a large scale.

> *The person who figures out how to harness the collective genius of the people in his or her organization is going to blow the competition away.*
> —Walter Wriston, CEO, former President,
> Citicorp/Citibank[11]

When employees are present with each other in the Here-Now, they experience a qualitative difference in their relationships. We already know that when individuals combine in common purpose to achieve a goal and work as a synergistic team, the sum of their energy is more than the sum of the individual energies involved. We have already accepted that in this situation 2 + 3 equal more than 5. If now, these same individuals combine in common purpose to achieve a goal while at the same time all are in the Here-Now, they form a new level of intelligence, which is called conjoined intelligence. Conjoined intelligence takes place when the joining of the intelligence of a group of individuals creates a new form of intelligence.

Employees are innovative, and creative solutions are found as needed. Any profound act of creation comes out of the state of being in the Here-Now. All of us can choose to be in the I Am. When employees are able to use time and space to access this place, they tap into their creative potential.

We know that we are holding the creative tension between goal achievement and possibilities when we have the qualitative evidence that employees are more energetic, clear and focused, resilient to change, have more productive work relationships, and are able to solve problems creatively.

The quantitative evidence of the successful application of the Self-Powerment Model is found in a healthier bottom line.

Seven

MUSINGS: GOING DEEPER

I f you have read this far to garner the information and do the practices necessary to integrate the principles of the Self-Powerment Model into your everyday life, you have certainly met the expectation of this author. However if, like me, you have become deeply intrigued with the possibilities of this shift to the Here-Now, I share some personal musings for your reflection. I welcome you to use them as starting points for your own musing. My suggestion is that you read only one muse at a time, reflect on it, and use the pages provided at the end of this chapter to record your own impressions.

To muse is to speculate voluntarily or enter a state of dreamy abstraction. When we muse, we take something that speaks to us and we willingly let go of the boundaries of the limited thinking mind, as we give ourselves over to the process of letting our inner compass guide us along. To muse is to speculate about possibilities. As such, it has the potential to expand our awareness of reality—of what is so. The question, "What if this is so?" can trigger many possible implications. To muse is to have no attachment to outcome, nor is outcome an intrinsic part of musing.

It is of great importance that the general public be given an opportunity to experience—consciously and intelligently—the efforts and results of scientific research. It is not sufficient that each result be taken up, elaborated and applied by a few specialists in the field. Restricting the body of knowledge to a small group deadens the philosophical spirit of a people and leads to spiritual poverty.

—Albert Einstein[12]

When I am in the I Am, I open to that place where time and space are relative and the information now known in quantum physics can be experienced in everyday life. Concepts like complementarity, non-local influence, wave-particle duality have all emerged as helpful tools for us lay folk to live with awareness. The intuitive nature of quantum physics can be achieved through the doorway of the I Am—where they are no longer concepts, but experiences.

Einstein did not set out to prove anything about the nature of our minds. His interest was in physics. The fact that he did illustrate something of importance about the way that we structure our perceptions is indicative of an inevitable trend toward the merger of physics and psychology.
—Gary Zukav, *The Dancing Wu Li Masters*[13]

One of the most exciting parts of the Self-Powerment Model is the intrinsic connection between psychology and physics. In order for me to appreciate this connection, I had to change the domain in which I saw physics. Instead of complex mathematical formulas presented in unfathomable symbols and equations, physics now expanded to the study of relationships, relativity of concepts, and possibilities. For example, the uncertainty principle states that we cannot observe something without changing it. There is no such thing as the independent observer who can stand on the sideline and watch nature run its course without influencing it. This reality has a great impact on our reliance on measurement as the most powerful tool for assessing real change.

Ken Wilber in *The Spectrum of Consciousness* states

> . . . *the point then, is not to confuse the world as it is with the world as it is measured into space, time, objects, classes, delineations, boundaries, limits, particulars, universals, individuals, generals, or categories of any type or kind—for the simple reason that all measurement is a product of thought not reality; just as for example, wood is not actually composed of inches but is only conventionally and mentally measured or divided into very arbitrary units called "inches."*[14]

What this means is that much of the quantitative data generated by the business world is really a product of what individual people choose to see and therefore choose to measure, and therefore choose to act upon—as if it were so.

Does this mean that quantitative measurement draws arbitrary conclusions because it totally depends upon the context created by the measurer?

In the current business context of Enron, WorldCom, and Arthur Andersen, to name but a few companies, drawing any conclusion based upon the quantitative financial picture painted of the Enrons and WorldComs is impossible or at best highly dangerous. It is not only a matter of what the individuals painting the picture choose to see, but also what they wish the viewer to see, regardless of the veracity of the ultimate picture.

When we think about something, we move in linear time; therefore, we cannot experience the present.

> *The present is not contained in thought. Thus, an analysis cannot actually cover the moment of analysis.*
> David Bohm—*On Dialogue*[15]

If we are paying attention to our thinking, we are not experiencing, and we can only experience in the I Am.

> *Surely, to be creative means to be in the state in which truth can come into being. And truth can come into being only when there is a complete cessation of the thought process.*
> —J. Krishnamurti[16]

We have learned to think about everything. Common wisdom cautions us to think before we speak, to think before we act. But as long as we're thinking, we're not experiencing. Take the small boy playing on the kitchen floor with a pot and a spoon. He is loving playing with the pot and spoon and isn't thinking, "Last week I wasn't as good a banger," or, "Next week, if I practice, I will be a better banger," or, "Sarah is a better banger than I," or, "I'll never be a good banger." He is just banging, loving it, and learning about life, as well. He's learning about how other people respond to his banging. He may discover, "Oops, if I bang too hard I make a dent in the pot," and through that experience he learns about pressure and force. He's learning a lot about reality without thinking about it.

Thinking has created the belief system that truth can be observed and measured—that it is somehow independent of the person observing the "truth." Quantum physics has now called that reality into question. Thinking is very useful for practical purposes. It also allows abstraction, which is necessary to create much of the technology we use every day. Abstraction, a subset of reality, is both useful and necessary, but not sufficient for allowing access to direct experience.

When we are grounded and centered in the Here-Now, we know the true meaning of nonattachment.

> *In this state of consciousness, the true meaning of non-attachment is apparent . . . It is simply that I am no longer attached to the need for things or events to be a certain way. I have let go of the belief that what goes on around me determines whether or not I am content.*
>
> —Peter Russell, *Waking Up in Time*[17]

We learn to experience life by creating an expectation of how we want things to be and then comparing the reality of what is to that expectation. Rarely do we just participate in reality as it is.

When we are attached to something—someone or an outcome—we cannot fully enter into experience. When we buy our new dream car, we get attached to it. When we teach, we get attached to our students. When we apply for a job, we are attached to getting it. When we fall in love, we get attached to our lover. Attachments come in the form of thought processes whose content sustain the need for the attachment. So in truth, we are not allowing ourselves to participate fully in the experience and address whatever the experience brings. We take energy from the experience to create the attachment. We pay a high price for attachments: we drain ourselves of energy. Since we create the attachment in the first place, we think we can control all the variables associated with it. When we begin to live the experience, we control only ourselves; therefore, the experience must be different.

In the Here-Now there is an intuitive understanding of the nature of paradox.

However, as long as paradox is treated as a problem, it can never be resolved.

David Bohm—*On Dialogue*[18]

When we experience life as a paradox, a whole new relationship to value emerges. So instead of looking at laziness as something to eliminate, we can see intrinsic value in it as a balance to the work ethic. If we responded to that ethic all the time, we would experience stress and eventual burnout. Paradox, then, allows for each part of life to be of service to the overall whole.

In her book, *The Quantum Self,* Dana Zohar[19] postulates that the origin of consciousness has a physical basis. She speaks about a state in which all the neurons vibrate in unison when at a certain frequency and calls this the blackboard of consciousness. Vibration is very difficult to notice when we are busy thinking. It has such a physical basis that a person must be "in tune" with the vibration to experience it. When we think without choice, we create static interference, which totally cuts off our ability to experience the rhythm of the universe both internally and externally.

When in the I Am, we experience our resonance with the environment, with other humans, and with ourselves. Can rhythm and vibrations possibly be the origin of both spirit and matter?

David Abram in the book *The Spell of the Sensuous* states that,

> *It is not writing per se, but phonetic writing and the Greek alphabet in particular, that enables the abstraction of previously ephemeral qualities like "goodness" and "justice" from their inherence in situations promoting them to a new realm independent of the flux of ordinary experience.*[20]

How can inherent qualities like goodness and justice be abstracted out of an experience?

Before there was language, if I wanted to describe or relate to you my experience of my cat, the actual cat had to be present. Once we create the word *cat,* which stands for the actual cat, then my actual cat no longer needs to be part of present experience for me to talk about it.

Before there was language, if a man took a piece of bread because his children were starving before his eyes, this situation had a very different meaning than the word *stealing* has in modern-day law.

Language allows concepts like goodness and justice to be

independent of what is happening Here-Now. Consequently, language cannot communicate the reality of what is so, only the abstraction of that reality.

Personal Musings

CONCLUSION

Exploration of awareness, how to access direct experience in the Here-Now, has been studied since ancient times, particularly through the writings and meditation practices of spiritual mystics and eastern religions. Humans have long been in search of that state where we can be truly and fully ourselves—in all our glory and potentiality.

Today, as never before, an increasingly large number of individuals all over the world are searching for ways to experience living in the Here-Now. We know that the wisdom gained from accessing and utilizing direct experience is no longer a luxury; in fact, it is requisite for our survival as a human species. How fitting that the modern science of quantum physics wed with modern psychology has pointed us to another gateway to the Here-Now at this pivotal time in human evolution—a gateway that is universally available to us all—right here, right now.

Once we witness how we almost always use time and space to structure our thoughts and language in ways that keep us out of the Here-Now, we can then consciously choose to reverse this process. When we change the structure of our language and thought to reflect the state of being in the Here-Now, we do nothing short of change our experience of reality.

By changing the structure of our language to the I Am, we change and expand our experience of reality. If we pay attention to the structure of our thoughts and language in the Here-Now, we can shift to experiencing the Here-Now. Can it be that simple? We can recognize truth by its beauty and simplicity. We can recognize the power of this Model by experiencing it.

When we live in the Here-Now, we are able to drop all human conditioning with its entrenched and limited thought patterns and start anew. What world can we create when we do this? A world of infinite possibility.

We can choose to reexamine our values and refocus on what has real meaning for us in our lives. We can choose to take action to create personal, work, and world environments that reflect our higher vision of what can be so. To take the most effective action, we need to draw not only from our ever-expanding cognitive abilities, but also from the wisdom that comes to us from direct experience in the Here-Now. Such fertile ground produces healthy and compassionate relationships with our environment, with other people and nations—but most important, with ourselves.

From Model to action—this is your choice.

Afterword

Self-Powerment reinforces the mission of Namaste Publishing, which is to publish only those books that celebrate the inestimable value of each individual. To all our readers I say, "Namasté."

Namasté is a word used to honor the light within, and is often spoken or written as a greeting or blessing. The extended meaning of the word has been written as "I honor the place in you in which the entire universe dwells. I honor the place in you which is of love, of truth, of light, and of peace. When you are in that place in you, and I am in that place in me, we are one."

Notes

1. Bohm, D. *On Dialogue.* New York: Routledge, 1996.
2. Zukav, G. *The Seat of the Soul.* New York: Simon & Schuster, 1990.
3. Tolle, E. *The Power of Now.* Novato, Calif.: New World Library, 1999.
4. Lorde, A. *Sister Outsider.* Freedom, Calif.: The Crossing Press, 1984.
5. Russell, P. *Waking Up in Time.* Novato, Calif.: Origin Press Inc., 1998.
6. Houston, J. *The Hero and the Goddess.* New York: Random House, 1992.
7. Zukav, G. *The Dancing Wu Li Masters.* New York: Morrow & Co., 1979.
8. Zukav, G. *The Seat of the Soul.* New York: Simon & Schuster, 1990.
9. McFarlane, T., Ed. *Einstein and Buddha: The Parallel Sayings.* Berkeley, Calif.: Ulysses Press, 2002.
10. Pritchett, P. *Carpe Mañana.* Texas: Pritchett Rummler-Brache, 2000.
11. Pritchett, P. *Carpe Mañana.* Texas: Pricthett Rummler-Brache, 2000.
12. Keller, L. "Science, observation, and mystery," *Parabola*, 25: 2, May 2000.
13. Zukav, G. *The Dancing Wu Li Masters.* New York: Morrow & Co., 1979.
14. Wilber, K. *The Collected Works of Ken Wilber.* Boston: Shambala, 1999.
15. Bohm, D. *On Dialogue.* New York: Routledge, 1996.
16. Krishnamurti, J. "Educating the educator." *Parabola.* 25: 3, August 2000.
17. Russell, P. *Waking Up in Time.* Novato, Calif.: Origin Press Inc., 1998.
18. Bohm, D. *On Dialogue.* New York: Routledge, 1996.
19. Zohar, D. *The Quantum Self.* New York: William Morrow & Co., 1990.
20. Abram, D. *The Spell of the Sensuous.* New York: Random House, 1996.

Glossary of Terms
in the Self-Powerment Model

Centered: Attention focused inside ourselves on our multisensory data.

Conditioning: Learned thought structures that take us away from the place of self-powerment.

Conjoined intelligence: When the joining of the intelligence of a group of individuals creates a new form of intelligence.

Direct experience: The quieting of thought to allow a full openness to experience.

Grounded: In the present moment.

Here-Now: The state of being in the present moment without attention to thought. Attention is focused internally on multi-sensory experience.

I Am: The way Here-Now is expressed in our language. The way we associate ourselves with time and space. The I Am defines us in time and space.

Intuition: The direct perception of the truth.

Ken: Range of site or vision; to have knowledge about, to know.

Negation: That which isn't.

Piggyback: To take a feeling and move it from the body on to a thought.

Self-Powerment: The state of being secure, in control, and adequate; using feelings to keep us in the present moment focused internally on our multisensory data.

Wisdom: Knowledge of what is true or right coupled with just judgment as to action, discernment, or insight.

Wobble: The state we are in when a life situation takes us out of the Here-Now.

Bibliography

Abram, D. *The Spell of the Sensuous.* New York: Random House, 1996.

Bohm, D. *On Dialogue.* New York: Routledge, 1996.

Capra, F. *The Web of Life.* New York: Random House, 1996.

———. *The Tao of Physics*, 4th ed. Boston: Shambala, 2000.

Cole, K. C. *First You Build a Cloud.* Orlando, Fla.: Harcourt Brace & Co., 1999.

DeMello, A. *Awareness.* New York: Doubleday, 1992.

Dossey, L. *Space, Time, and Medicine.* Boulder, Colo.: Shambala, 1982.

Edelman, G. and G. Tononi. *A Universe of Consciousness.* New York: Basic Books, 2000.

Elgin, D. *Awakening Earth.* New York: William Morrow & Co., 1993.

Houston, J. *The Hero and the Goddess.* New York: Random House, 1992.

Keller, L. "Science, Observation, and Mystery." *Parabola.* 25: 2, May 2000.

Krishnamurti, J. "Educating the Educator." *Parabola.* 25: 3, August 2000.

Lorde, A. *Sister Outsider.* Calif.: The Crossing Press, 1984.

McFarlane, T. Ed. *Einstein & Buddha: The Parallel Sayings.* Calif.: Ulysses Press, 2002.

Pritchett, P. *Carpe Mañana.* Texas: Pritchett Rummer-Brache, 2000.

Rickman, John. Ed. *A General Selection from Works of Sigmund Freud.* New York: Doubleday & Co. Inc., 1957.

Russell, P. *Waking Up in Time.* Novato, Calif.: Origin Press Inc., 1998.

Thomas, L. *The Lives of a Cell.* New York: Penguin Books, 1978.

About the Author

FAYE MANDELL has a Ph.D. in Counseling Psychology from Boston College. She travels extensively, leading workshops throughout the country. Her clients include several Fortune 500 companies. Dr. Mandell lives with her three children in Providence, Rhode Island.

CONTACT INFORMATION

Namaste Publishing Inc.

P.O. Box 62084   Vancouver, B.C.   Canada V6J 1Z1
Telephone: 604-224-3179   Fax: 604-224-3354
E-mail: namaste@telus.net   www.namastepublishing.com

For information on scheduled public talks and teachings given by
Faye Mandell and other Namaste Publishing authors:
www.namastepublishing.com

To inquire about or book Faye Mandell or other Namaste Publishing
authors for a teaching or speaking engagement, contact:

Kathy Cholod – Namaste Teachings
Telephone: 604-261-3137 (PST)   Fax: 604-224-3354
E-mail: namaste3@telus.net

To place an order for SELF-POWERMENT by Faye Mandell
or other Namaste publications, visit our online bookstore:

www.namastepublishing.com

or Contact Nora Morin – Namaste Productions
Telephone: 250-954-1693 (PST)   Fax: 250-248-2198
E-mail: namaste@shaw.ca